むずかしい教えがスッキリわかる！
英語対訳で読む禅入門

尾関宗園 Souen Ozeki 監修

Elizabeth Mills 英文監訳

実業之日本社

Zen is one of the most important fundamentals of Japanese culture. It influenced so many aspects of Japanese life that even non-Buddhists have the "mind of Zen". However, since some Buddhist terms are difficult to understand, Zen is not popular among us.

Originally, the teaching of Zen was to explain and teach the way of life easily to the people. The phrases of Priest Souen Ozeki, which we quote in chapter one, suggest the way to live with very simple and easy words according to Zen teaching. We present an introduction to Zen.

When we started to write this book, we were bewildered by the difficulty in translation. Soon, we became aware that the cause of the difficulty was in the words which had been translated from Sanskrit to archaic Chinese, and then to archaic Japanese. Thereafter, we worked to understand the terms, keeping in mind the original meaning of the Chinese symbols. Then we found that, in many cases, the English translation of the Chinese characters was easier to understand than those of the Japanese words both for Japanese and English natives.

Although Zen is thought to be difficult to translate into English, with the assistance of Elizabeth Mills, we completed the English section with simple phrases using basic words. We also intend to produce a text which will enable native English speakers to understand the comprehensive aspects of Zen. We hope that the knowledge of Zen provided in this book will help native English speakers, who are interested in Japanese culture, to understand the framework of Zen, as well as Japanese who are interested in English language and Zen.

PREFACE / はじめに

　禅は、日本文化の基礎をなす重要な要素の一つです。その影響はあまりにも大きく、仏教を信仰しない日本人でさえも、少なからず影響を受けているといえます。しかし、仏教の言葉は難解であるということもあり、それほど身近に感じることができません。

　禅の教えは、本来、やさしくわかりやすい言葉で、人間のあり方を人々に説くものであったはずです。本書の第一章にある尾関宗園和尚の言葉は、禅の教えからわかりやすく人が生きる道を説いています。そうした意味でも、本書はまさしく「禅の入門書」といえるでしょう。

　私たちが、この本をつくり始めたとき、まず禅語の英訳の難しさに戸惑いました。しばらくして、その原因は仏教語がサンスクリット語から漢語に訳され、それが日本語に訳されたからではないかと思うようになりました。それ以降、できるだけ漢字の意味を理解し、それを英訳するように心がけました。漢字の意味をそのまま英訳すると、英語を母国語とする人々だけでなく、日本人にも原意が理解しやすくなることが多いようです。

　本書は、英文監訳者のエリザベス・ミルズさんの協力を得て、英語では説明しにくいと思われがちである「禅」を英語の基礎単語を使い、読みやすい構文で説明しています。もちろん、ネイティブ・スピーカーが読んでも禅の全体像がつかめるような英文にするよう、心がけました。そうした意味からも、英語と禅に関心を持つ日本人のみならず、日本文化に興味を持つ外国人の皆さんにも、禅に対する理解を深める一助にしていただければ幸いです。

第 1 章　宗園和尚が説く禅の心
/ Priest Souen's Sermons of Zen's Mind　　9

1. 禅とは何か / What is Zen?　　10
2. 自分を助けてくれるものは何か?
　　　　　　　/ What Things Will Help You in Your Life?　12
3. 仕事をするのは何のため? / Why Should We Work?　14
4. がむしゃらに一所懸命に打ち込む / Put Your All into Your Work　16
5. 人はなぜ学ばなければならないのか?
　　　　　　　　　/ Why Do We Have to Study?　18
6. あなたが一番えらいのです! / You Are the Greatest!　20
7. 辛い、苦しい、悲しいとき
　　　　　　/ When You Feel Pain, Agony or Sadness…　22
8. 「いま、ここ」に集中する / Concentrating on Here and Now　24
9. 老いることはどんどん捨てること / To Age Is to Strip Away　26
10. 「死」は誰にもわからないこと / Death Is What Nobody Knows　28
▶ 中国禅師年表 / Chinese Zen Masters Chronology　30

第 2 章　禅の歴史 / History of Zen　　31

11. 釈迦(しゃか)は坐禅をして悟りを開いた
　　　　　　/ Gautama Siddhārtha Achieves Enlightenment　32
12. 禅の始まり「拈華微笑(ねんげみしょう)」
　　　　　　　/ The Beginning of Zen, "The Flower Sermon"　34
13. 禅は達磨大師(だるまだいし)がインドから中国へ伝えた
　　/ Zen Was Transmitted from India to China by Bodhidharma　36
14. 達磨の禅 / Bodhidharma's Zen　38
15. 達磨と慧可(えか) / Bodhidharma and Eka　40
16. 慧能(えのう)の禅 / Enō's Zen　42
17. 馬祖(ばそ)と百丈(ひゃくじょう) / Baso and Hyakujō　44
18. 日本の禅① / Zen in Japan ①　46
19. 日本の禅② / Zen in Japan ②　48

CONTENTS / 目次

20. 三つの禅宗 / Three Zen Schools	50
▶禅の影響を受けた人々① 松尾芭蕉 / Matsuo Bashō	52

第3章　禅の修行 / Zen's Practices　53

21. 禅の修行とは / What is Zen Training?	54
22. 僧として修行するには / How to Become a Priest	56
23. 僧堂に入門するまで / Before Entering the Monastery	58
24. 雲水の修行生活 / Training Life of Unsui	60
25. 僧堂における坐禅の作法 / Manner of Zazen in Monastery	64
26. 坐禅の組み方 / How to Do Zazen	66
27. 姿勢の調え方と呼吸法 / The Posture of Zazen and Breathing	70
28. 警策の受け方と坐禅の終え方 / How to Be Hit with Keisaku and Finish Zazen	72
29. 読経について / Reciting Sutras	76
▶般若心経 / Heart Sutra	78
▶禅の影響を受けた人々② 井伊直弼 / Ii Naosuke	80

第4章　『十牛図』を読み解く / Interpretation of Ten Bulls　81

30.『十牛図』とは何か? / What is "Ten Bulls"?	82
31. 第一図「尋牛」/ No.1 "Searching for the Bull"	84
32. 第二図「見跡」/ No.2 "Discovering the Footprints"	86
33. 第三図「見牛」/ No.3 "Perceiving the Bull"	88
34. 第四図「得牛」/ No.4 "Catching the Bull"	90
35. 第五図「牧牛」/ No.5 "Taming the Bull"	92
36. 第六図「騎牛帰家」/ No.6 "Riding the Bull Home"	94
37. 第七図「忘牛存人」/ No.7 "The Bull Transcended"	96
38. 第八図「人牛俱忘」/ No.8 "Both Bull and Self Transcended"	98
39. 第九図「返本還源」/ No.9 "Reaching the Source"	100
40. 第十図「入鄽垂手」/ No.10 "In the World"	102
▶禅の影響を受けた人々③ 三遊亭圓朝 / San-yūtei Enchō	104

第5章 「公案」を読む / Reading Kōan　　　　　　　　　　105

41. 公案とは / What is Kōan?　106
42. 狗子仏性（『無門関』一則）/ Joshū's Dog　108
43. 趙州洗鉢（『無門関』七則）/ Joshū Washes a Bowl　110
44. 百丈野狐（『無門関』二則）/ Hyakujō's Wild Fox　112
45. 南泉斬猫（『無門関』十四則）/ Nansen Cuts the Cat in Two　114
46. 庭前柏樹（『無門関』三十七則）/ The Juniper Tree in Front of the Hall　116
47. 竿頭進歩（『無門関』四十六則）/ Progress from the Top of the Pole　118
48. 馬大師不安（『碧巌録』三則）/ Master Baso Is Ill　120
49. 洞山無寒暑（『碧巌録』四十三則）/ Tōzan's "Cold and Heat"　122
50. 非風非幡（『無門関』二十九則）/ Not the Wind, Not the Flag　124
51. 奚仲造車（『無門関』八則）/ Keichū Makes a Cart　126
52. 隻手音声（『白隠禅師坐禅和讃』）/ The Sound of One Hand　128
▶ 禅の影響を受けた人々④　夏目漱石 Natsume Sōseki　130

第6章 禅のことば / Zen's Words　　　　　　　　　　131

53. 不立文字と教外別伝
　/ Communication Without Words, a Lesson Without Teaching　132
54. 直指人心と見性成仏
　/ Seize Your "Mind of Buddha", Be Aware of Your "Mind of Buddha"　134
55. 主人公 / Hero　136
56. 只管打坐 / Wrestle in Sitting　138
57. 一行三昧 / Samadhi of One Practice　140
58. 放下著 / Let It Go　142
59. 一日不作一日不食（いちじつなさざれば　いちじつくらわず）
　　　　　　/ A Day Without Work, Is a Day Without Eating　144
60. 日日是好日 / Everyday Is a Good Day　146
61. 本来の面目 / The True Face　148
62. 喫茶去 / Have a Cup of Tea　150
63. 平常心是道 / The Neutral Mind Is the Way　152

CONTENTS / 目次

64. 少欲知足 / Desire Little and Know Contentment		154
▶ 日本禅師年表 / Japanese Zen Masters Chronology		156

第7章　禅師たちのプロフィール / Profile of Zen Masters　157

65. 栄西 (1141~1215) / Myōan Eisai		158
66. 道元 (1200~1253) / Dōgen		160
67. 一休 宗純 (1394~1481) / Ikkyū Sōjun		162
68. 沢庵 宗彭 (1573~1646) / Takuan Sōhō		164
69. 鈴木 正三 (1579~1655) / Suzuki Shōzan		166
70. 隠元 隆琦 (1592~1673) / Ingen Ryūki		168
71. 白隠 慧鶴 (1685~1768) / Hakuin Ekaku		170
72. 大愚 良寛 (1758~1831) / Taigu Ryōkan		172
73. 鈴木 大拙 (1870~1966) / Suzuki Daisetsu		174
▶ 禅の影響を受けた人々⑤　スティーブ・ジョブズ / Steve Jobs		176

第8章　禅と日本文化の関わり / Zen and Japanese Culture　177

74. 禅と芸術 / Zen and Japanese Art		178
75. 茶道 / Tea Ceremony		180
76. 禅と剣の道 / Zen and the Swordsmanship		182
77. 書道 / Japanese Calligraphy		184
78. 水墨画 / Wash Painting		186
79. 禅庭 / Zen Garden		188
80. 精進料理 / Buddhist Cuisine		190

装幀	杉本 欣右
イラスト	笹森 識
執筆	森井 美紀
編集・英訳	中村 英良
DTP	スタジオスパーク

Terms used in Buddhism/ 仏教語

[本書でよく出てくる仏教語]

仏教 / Buddhism
仏陀 / Buddha
仏心 / mind of Buddha
仏性 / Buddhist nature
仏道 / the way of Buddha
成仏する / become a Buddha
禅 / Zen
坐禅 / zazen
禅師 / Zen master
僧侶 / a priest
出家する / become a priest
弟子 / a disciple
修行 / training
参禅する / practice Zen
僧堂 / a monastery
衣鉢 / a robe and a bowl
宗派 / school
悟りを開く / attain enlightenment
大悟する / attain great enlightenment
印可 / certification or master's approval
公案 / "kōan" or a question given by master to attain enlightenment
無 / "mu" or nothingness
空 / emptiness
分別 / differenciation

真理 / truth
精進する / devote oneself
智慧 / wisdom
境地 / the ultimate stage
托鉢 / religious begging
布施 / offering
勤行 / labors
作務 / routine work as cleaning
因果の法則 / the rule of causality
説法 / preaching/sermon
妄想 / delusion
苦悩 / suffering
苦行 / penance
合掌する / put your palms together
低頭する / bow low
読経する / recite the sutra
禅定 / "Dhyāna", "zenjyo" or meditate and concentrate the mind to see the truth
三昧 / "Samadhi", "zanmai" or devotion to a particular thing
煩悩 / "kleasa", "bon-no" or actions which disturb body and mind such as desire

Chapter 1

Priest Souen's Sermons of Zen's Mind

第1章

宗園和尚が説く禅の心

Zen Buddhism

1 What Is Zen?

①You may have an impression that Zen is a way to achieve a deep silence of the mind. ②In other words, you might think Zen preaches a way to escape from your daily life. ③Zen is not so much a way to feel at peace but a way to reach the "mind of Buddha". ④The "mind of Buddha" or "enlightenment" is something which everybody has, that exists deep within one's mind.
⑤The aim of Zen practice is to find this Buddhist nature within one's self, through zazen and practice of Buddha's teachings.
⑥The more you know the Buddhist nature, the more you recognize, all that you thought was important, is in reality, trivial. ⑦As your viewpoint or mindset changes, then your way of living changes.
⑧Whenever someone asks me what Zen is, I reply as follows:

第1章　宗園和尚が説く禅の心

⑨"Zen is to know the frame of mind. ⑩It is the mettle to take a look at oneself and come to grips with reality. ⑪It is Zen that cultivates the mettle."
⑫Zen's essence both reveals the way you are and polishes your mind throughout daily life.

1. 禅とは何か

①禅とは心の静寂を得るためのもの、という印象を持っている人がいるかもしれません。②もしくは、現実から少し離れて超然とするための教えと思っている人もいるかもしれません。③禅は、そのようなものではなく、仏心に近づくための道程のことです。④仏心とは、悟りの境地のことで、人の心の中にあります。⑤禅を修行する目的とは、坐禅と釈迦の教えを通して、自分の中にある仏性を見つけることです。⑥仏性を知れば、それまで大事だと思っていたことが、実はとるに足らないものであることがわかります。⑦ものの見方が変わり、生き方が変わります。

⑧「禅とは何ですか」と聞かれたら、私はこう答えます。

⑨「それは心の持ち方である。⑩自分自身を見つめ、精一杯現実に立ち向かっていく気概である。⑪それを養うことが禅の役目だ」と。⑫禅の本質は、ありのままの自分の姿をさらけ出し、日常を通して心を磨くことです。

2 What Things Will Help You in Your Life?

① You should be happy to answer "my heart", when asked if you know a person who feels warmly about you.
② It is only your heart that wholeheartedly helps you and thinks of you when you are forced into a corner.
③ So, you should keep your heart pure. ④ An unclear or unclean heart gets in the way of making the right decision.
⑤ A hard and unbending heart might easily be shattered.
⑥ You can change the condition of your heart by nurturing it daily.

⑦ Keep your heart like a stream, burbling through deep mountains, refreshed and open wide without any debris, so that you will never be forced into a corner.
⑧ "Self-Help" was a best-seller in

the United States. ⑨I think that the well known phrase of
　　　　　　　　　　　　　　　　　　　有名な　　　　　一文
the author Samuel Smiles, "Heaven helps those who help

themselves", is related to the "mind of Zen".
　　　　　　　～に関係している

2. 自分を助けてくれるものは何か？

①「あなたの身になって考えてくれる人をご存知ですか」と、もし聞かれたら、「自分の心です」と答えられたら、いいですね。
②自分が窮地に陥ったときに、自分を一番親身になって助けたり思いやってくれるのは「自分の心」をおいてはほかにありません。③ですから、いつも心をぴかぴかにしておくといいのです。④心が曇っていたり汚れていたりすると、正しい判断ができません。⑤心がこわばってカチカチになっていると、簡単に砕けてしまうかもしれません。⑥心の状態は、日常の修養で変えることができるのです。
⑦さらさら流れる山間の清流のような心になり、ガラクタなどなく、すっきりして広々とした心を保っていると、窮地に陥るようなことすらもなくなるのではないでしょうか。
⑧アメリカのベストセラー書に『自助論』という本があります。
⑨作者のサミュエル・スマイルズの「天は自ら助くる者を助く」という有名な一文がありますが、その考え方は、禅の精神に通じていると思います。

3 Why Should We Work?

①Keeping your heart clean and open, you will approach the
近づく
"mind of Buddha". ②All the things surrounding you in
仏心   周りを取り囲む
your daily life could become paths to finding your heart.
日常生活   探す道
③Your work is the best place to think about the way to live
              絶好の場所
as a human being and to practice it.
     人間   実践する
④You should undertake your work to find the "mind of
             取り組む
Buddha" which exists in yourself.
              ～に存在する
⑤You should have the sense that you were given your life
                    感覚   命を与えられた
to carry out the work.
取り組む
⑥You should continue to carry out the work you are faced
             ～し続ける   実行する   ～に直面する
with, wholeheartedly and with determination. ⑦As a result
       誠心誠意で   意を決して(→腹をくくって)   ～の結果として
of striving to master the way, you will get close to the truth.
 懸命に努力すること 究める   ～に近づく   真実
⑧If you are close to the truth, you do not have to care what
                                    気にする必要はない
people think of you. ⑨All you have to do is to expose your
                    あなたがしなければならないことは   さらけ出す
nature as it is.
ありのままの姿
⑩To devote yourself is to show single-mindedly a
   一所懸命に打ち込むこと(→精進すること)   ひたすら

14

passionate attitude
熱心な態度（→自己を燃焼させる姿勢）

3. 仕事をするのは何のため？

①心をきれいにし、広々とさせておくと仏心に近づいていきます。②日常のすべてが心を探す道になります。

③仕事は「人間が人間として生きる道とは何か」ということを考えたり、実践したりする絶好の場です。

④自分の中にある仏心に出会うために、仕事に取り組むのです。

⑤この仕事をするために、私は命をもらったという感覚でやるといいのです。

⑥いま直面している仕事に、誠心誠意で腹をくくって取り組み続けることです。⑦その道を究めるという修行をした結果、真実に近づけるのです。

⑧そうして真実に近づけば、他人の評価など気にすることはありません。⑨ありのままの姿をさらけ出せばいいのです。

⑩精進するということは、ひたすら自己を燃焼させる姿勢のことです。

4 Put Your All into Your Work

①When you think it is the right work for you, you should challenge it in your own way – even if you are beaten and hurt.

②From beginning to end, Zen practice is to concentrate on the matter before your eyes. ③Do not think this or that; just concentrate. ④As a result, you will see the "mind of Buddha".

⑤A non-priest also can find a way if you tackle the matter before your eyes with whole heart and mind and strength.

⑥You should do immediately what you think is right with all your power.

⑦That becomes the true way of yourself. ⑧The way will become more polished as you train

yourself.

⑨Your future exists at this very moment. ⑩Life is a series
　　　未来　　exists　　まさにこの瞬間　　　　　　　連続
of "these moments" which you are content with and you
　　　　　　　　　　　　　　　　　　～に満足する
strive for.
懸命に努力する

---

4. がむしゃらに一所懸命に打ち込む

①自分が正しいと思う仕事なら、叩かれようが傷つこうがマイペースでぶつかっていくことが大事です。

②禅の修行はとにかく目の前のことに没頭することに終始します。③頭であれこれ考えず、ただ集中するのみ。④その結果、仏心に出会えるわけです。

⑤一般の人も、目の前のことに全身全霊をかけてぶつかることで、活路が見出せるのです。⑥正しいと思ったことは、いますぐ全力ですぐやることです。

⑦それがその人の本当の「道」になります。⑧その道は、自らを鍛えることで磨きがかかります。⑨自分自身の将来は、「いま、この瞬間」にあるのです。

⑩「いま」をがんばり、「いま」を喜ぶ瞬間の連続が人生なのです。

5   Why Do We Have to Study?

①Each of us has a way to live our life. ②The way to live exists inside of ourselves. ③The most important thing is that you make your heart proceed step by step. ④The way is built with each step. ⑤You should start with recognizing this process and continue to study for your whole life. ⑥Fundamentally, study, is to raise your ability to contribute toward other people. ⑦Study continues until you die. ⑧If you live without creating your own way nor practicing the way, you will die without knowing the meaning of study and life.

⑨Study reminds us of the word knowledge. ⑩Knowledge means understanding the process of matters. ⑪In Buddhism, wisdom has a function which makes truth clear and helps us attain enlightenment. ⑫Studying is not only to gain knowledge but also to lead someone to wisdom.

第1章　宗園和尚が説く禅の心

5. 人はなぜ学ばなければならないのか？

①人にはそれぞれの「生きる道」があります。②その生きる道は自分の中にあります。③大切なことは、自分の心を一歩一歩自分で前へ前へと進めていくことです。④その一歩一歩が道になります。⑤それを認識(にんしき)することから学びが始まり、一生をかけて学ぶのです。

⑥本来、自分が持っている能力をどんどん高めて、よい行ないを他に施(ほどこ)すことが学びです。⑦死ぬまで学びの連続です。⑧道を切り開くこともなく、実践(じっせん)することもない人生ならば、学ぶことも生きる意味も知らないまま死んでしまうだけです。

⑨学ぶということから「知恵」という言葉が浮かびます。⑩知恵というのは、物事の道筋(みちすじ)を知ることです。⑪仏教でいう「智慧(ちえ)」は真理を明らかにし、悟りを開く働きのことです。

⑫学ぶということは、知恵を得るだけではなく、人を智慧に導くことでもあるのです。

6 You Are the Greatest!

①"In Heaven and Earth, only I, am the one to be respected"; this is the phrase *Gautama Siddhārtha* announced when he was born. ②"Heaven and Earth" point to the "great universe". ③This means that 'I', having been born miraculously, life should be very precious. ④Since "My life" is precious, you will learn that the life of all creatures is precious.

⑤All things are to be respected; myself and strangers, the present and the future, mankind and all creatures, without differentiation. ⑥The nature of life is to grow powerfully and strongly. ⑦We have one life, therefore cherish life and all its possibilities.

⑧We can not afford to be indecisive and worrisome. ⑨Think, so as not to be overcome by yourself and your weaknesses, and live decisively. ⑩Let us tackle matters head-on even if they are trivial. ⑪The reward lies in the

第1章　宗園和尚が説く禅の心

intent to undertake the challenge.
意思　　　取り組む

6. あなたが一番えらいのです！

①「天上天下唯我独尊」は釈迦が誕生したときに言ったとされる言葉です。②天上天下とは、大宇宙のことを指しています。③その中で奇跡のように生まれた生命である「我」は、とても尊いということを表現しています。④自分の命が尊いということから、あらゆるものの命が尊いということを知るのです。
⑤自分と他人、過去と未来、人間とそのほかの生物との差別もない、すべてのものが「唯我独尊」です。
⑥生命の本質は、より強くたくましく成長することにあります。
⑦だから、自分の生命と可能性を大切にして1回限りの人生を精一杯生きるのです。
⑧うじうじしたり、くよくよしたりする暇はありません。
⑨自分に負けないことだけ考えて徹底的に生きるのです。
⑩くだらないことにも真正面から取り組んでみましょう。⑪それに挑むという意思こそが宝物なのです。

21

7 When You Feel Pain, Agony or Sadness…

①The agony you have now is born in your mind. ②People have, inside themselves, the ability to resolve their troubles. ③Like all matters which have both negative and positive sides, there are both sides in the heart of people. ④It is up to the individual to select the side, positive or negative to "light up". ⑤If you change your view point, the two sides could be reversed.

⑥When you are troubled, you should face it with all your might. ⑦Then relax your heart and change your position a little. ⑧Having said that, there are cases where you can do nothing. ⑨When you have a disaster for example, there is no way. ⑩In the *Edo* period, *Ryōkan*, having experienced the Great *Echigo* earthquake, wrote to his friend as follows. ⑪"When you have a disaster, accept it. ⑫When you are dying, accept your death. ⑬This is the only way to escape from the disaster." ⑭If there is nothing you can do within your means, recognize this, and still, jump into the midst of the disaster. ⑮If you accept this, no more disaster will fall upon you. ⑯The way things are, will be changed if you let your heart be free.

7. 辛い、苦しい、悲しいとき

①いまの苦悩はあなたの心の中で生まれたものです。②人間は自らのうちに、問題を解決できる能力を持っています。③物事には陰と陽が在るように、人の心にもまた陰陽があります。④どちらの面を照らしているかは自分しだいなのです。⑤視点を変えることで、物事の陰陽が逆転します。

⑥悩んでいるときには、思い切り正面から悩みに向かい合いましょう。⑦そして自分の心の力を抜いて、自分の立ち位置を変えるのです。⑧そうは言っても、どうしようもないときもあるでしょう。⑨たとえば、災難に逢ったときは、自分ではどうしようもありません。⑩江戸時代、越後の大地震のときに、良寛は友人への手紙にこのように書きました。⑪「災難に遭うときは災難に遭うのがよい。⑫死ぬときは死ぬのがよい。⑬これが災難を逃れる方法である」と。⑭自力ではどうしようもないことは、それを認め、その渦中に飛び込んでいく。⑮すべてを受け入れると、それ以上の災難は降りかかってこないのです。⑯心を自在にすることで、周りのありようは変わるのです。

8 Concentrating on Here and Now

①People who are attached to the past and who anticipate the future are said not to be alive. ②To live is to be satisfied in the moment. ③Meaningful life is not one influenced by the future and the past, in other words, the life where you are not influenced by another person.

④A series of dots comprises a line. ⑤If this moment, as a dot, is not satisfied, the life, as a line, is not able to be satisfied.

⑥If you hope to be happy someday, you will never be happy. ⑦Only the person who feels happy here and now can continue to live with happiness.
⑧Therefore you should practice what you think is right concentrating on here and now. ⑨The important thing is to let yourself bloom at the place where you are at now.
⑩All things are changing from one hour to the next.
⑪Don't look to the past or worry about the future.

⑫Your life is the place you should train everyday.
訓練する

8.「いま、ここ」に集中する

①過去にこだわる人や未来に期待する人は、生きているとはいえません。②生きるとはその瞬間の充実です。③生きがいのある人生とは、過去とか未来にとらわれない人生のことで、言葉をかえれば、相手を気にする必要のない人生ということです。
④点の連続によって線ができます。⑤点であるその瞬間が充実していなければ、線である人生の充実はないのです。
⑥「いつか幸せになりたい」と願っている人には幸せはやって来ません。⑦「いま、ここ」で幸せを感じる人が、幸せをつかんで生きている人なのです。
⑧ですから、自分が正しいと思ったことは、「いま、ここ」に集中して即実行すること。⑨いま自分が置かれているところで、いかにして自分の花を咲かせるかが大事なのです。
⑩すべてのものは刻々と変化しています。⑪過去を振り返らず、未来を思い悩まないこと。
⑫自分の人生が、修行の場であり、毎日が修行の連続なのです。

9 To Age Is to Strip Away

①A human is born as a perfect being, pure and innocent without any desire or attachment to anything. ②We become corrupted as we are getting older, having gained experience and various professional titles, and being in messy human relationships. ③We lose the innocence we were born with, without knowing it, and become unconscious of the impurities which saturate our body.

④To age means to become conscious of the impurities. ⑤As you age, titles and relationships are not useful any longer, and the impurities and junk which you possess, rise to the surface.

⑥Let us strip these away, one by one. ⑦Chip away the impurities and recover the pure mind of a newborn baby. ⑧Let us strip away differentiation and ego, and live at your own pace.

⑨If you have a free mind, one which is not influenced by

第1章　宗園和尚が説く禅の心

anything, neither to live nor to die will terrify you any
　　　　　～も…も―することはない　　　　　　　恐れさせる　　もはや
longer.

9. 老いることはどんどん捨てること

①人間は純粋無垢（むく）で欲望や執着のかけらもない完璧な存在で生まれてきます。②年を重ねるにつれ、経験が増し、いろいろな肩書きが増え、人間関係が複雑になり、どんどん汚れていきます。③知らず知らずのうちに生まれたときの純粋さがなくなり、汚れが染みついていることにも気がつかなくなります。

④しかし、老いるということは、その汚れに気がつくようになることです。⑤年をとり、肩書きも人間関係もなくなると、いままで心の中に持っていたガラクタや汚れが浮き上がってきます。⑥それらを一つずつ、捨てていきましょう。⑦そぎ落として、生まれたころの純粋さに戻るのです。

⑧分別（ふんべつ）も我（が）も捨て、マイペースに生きていきましょう。

⑨何ものにもとらわれない自由な心になると「生」も「死」も怖くなくなります。

10 Death Is What Nobody Knows

①Does the world after death really exist? ②I do not know since I have never seen it. ③There is no reason to think about whether it exists or not, because nobody knows. ④There is no question that everybody must die. ⑤Zen master *Takuan* even mentioned that "you should believe that you were born in this world with the purpose to die". ⑥Even if life is a step by step walk to death, we are born again and again with the rising sun every morning. ⑦If you remember this, you will not be caught in a trap of thinking that death is terrible. ⑧If you live your life devoting yourself to the task at hand, you do not have the time to consider "what will come if I die". ⑨Since people do not grasp the reality about death when they are young, many young people can not attain any object. ⑩You should dare to set death beside you and live with the feeling that you have died once. ⑪Don't

escape from various matters, opposite them face to face and
<u>～から逃げる</u> <u>～に向かって</u> <u>正面きって</u>
live as well as possible. ⑫There is a Zen phrases which
<u>可能な限り（→精一杯）</u>
says "life and death seem to be one". ⑬<u>So to say</u>, "attain to
<u>いわば</u>
live" means "attain to die".

10.「死」は誰にもわからないこと

①「死後の世界」はあるのでしょうか。②私は見たことがないのでわかりません。③わからないことを、あるかないかと考えても仕方がありません。④誰もが必ず「死ぬ」ことは決まっています。⑤沢庵禅師は「この世には、死にに来たのだと思いなさい」とまで言っています。⑥死に向かって一歩ずつ歩いていくのが人生だとしても、私たちは毎朝太陽とともに、日々生まれ変わっているのです。⑦これを忘れなければ、「死は恐ろしい」という罠にはまることはないのです。

⑧毎日、目の前のことに必死になっていれば、「死んだらどうなる？」などと言っている暇はありません。⑨まだ若いうちは、「自分が死ぬ」ことにリアリティがありませんから、何事もやり遂げることができない人が多いのです。⑩あえて死を傍らに置き、いったん死んだ気になって生きてみることです。⑪もろもろのことに逃げないで正面から向き合い、精一杯生きるのです。⑫「生死一如」という禅の言葉があります。⑬「生ききる」ことは、「死にきる」ことなのです。

Chinese Zen Masters Chronology / 中国禅師年表

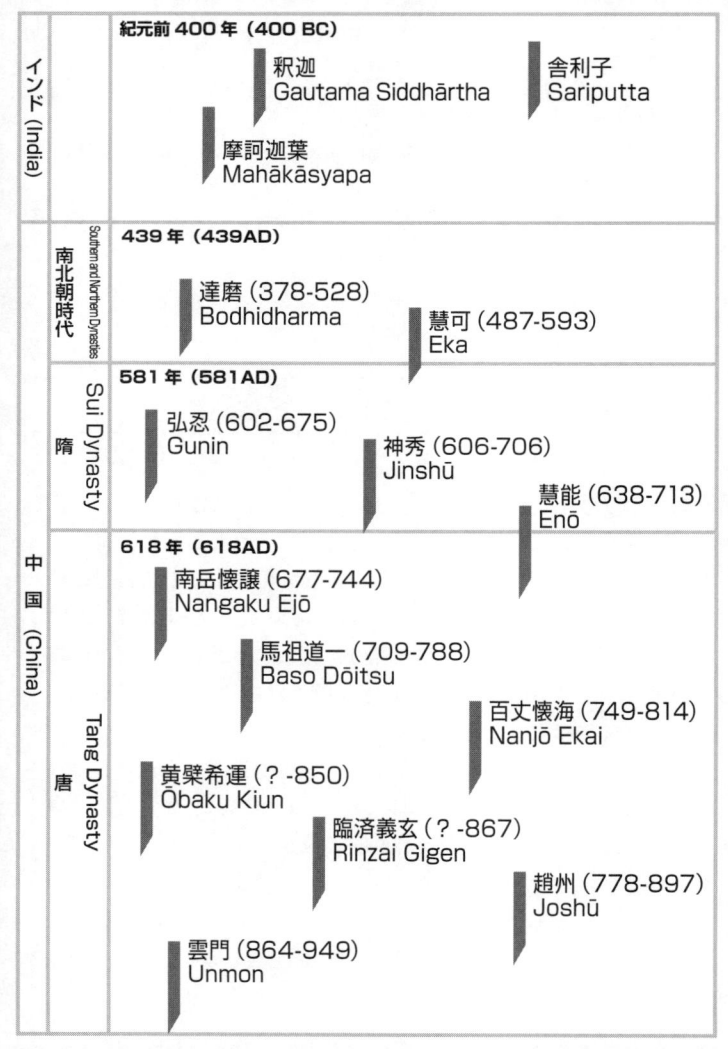

インド (India)		**紀元前 400 年 (400 BC)** 釈迦 Gautama Siddhārtha 舎利子 Sariputta 摩訶迦葉 Mahākāsyapa
中 国 (China)	南北朝時代 Southern and Northern Dynasties	**439 年 (439AD)** 達磨 (378-528) Bodhidharma 慧可 (487-593) Eka
	隋 Sui Dynasty	**581 年 (581AD)** 弘忍 (602-675) Gunin 神秀 (606-706) Jinshū 慧能 (638-713) Enō
	唐 Tang Dynasty	**618 年 (618AD)** 南岳懐譲 (677-744) Nangaku Ejō 馬祖道一 (709-788) Baso Dōitsu 百丈懐海 (749-814) Nanjō Ekai 黄檗希運 (?-850) Ōbaku Kiun 臨済義玄 (?-867) Rinzai Gigen 趙州 (778-897) Joshū 雲門 (864-949) Unmon

Chapter 2

History of Zen

第 2 章
禅の歴史

Zen Buddhism

11 *Gautama Siddhārtha* Achieves Enlightenment

①The founder of Buddhism, *Gautama Siddhārtha*, was born as a rich prince in northern India. ②Around the four gates located on the east, west, south, and north side of the castle, many people were suffering because of birth, old age, disease, and death. ③This suffering of the people worried him. ④Beyond these four sufferings, there were four more pains that troubled people: the pain of separation from loved ones, the pain of contact with hated ones, the frustration of unsatisfied desires, and five pains derived from body and mind. ⑤To escape from these eight sufferings, *Gautama* became a priest. ⑥Whether the Buddha was a rich prince or was bearing penance, he had not been able to reduce his suffering. ⑦Finally he noticed that following a path of moderation was the best, one away from the extremes of self-indulgence and self-mortification.

⑧Around 2500 years ago, when *Gautama* was practicing zazen under the *Bodhi* Tree located in *Bodh Gaya*, in easten India, he achieved enlightenment. ⑨Zazen had existed in India as a form of penance before Buddhism existed. ⑩Zazen became a part of Buddhism when *Gautama* attained enlightenment while he was practicing zazen.

11. 釈迦は坐禅をして悟りを開いた

①仏教の開祖・釈迦は、もともとインド北部の裕福な王子でした。②あるとき、城の東西南北の四つの門にいた人たちが、「生老病死」で苦しんでいました。③彼はその姿を見て悩みました。④その四つの苦に、「愛別離苦（愛する人と別れる苦しみ）」、「怨憎会苦（憎む人と会う苦しみ）」、「求不得苦（欲しいものが手に入らない苦しみ）」、「五蘊盛苦（体や心から生まれる五つの苦しみ）」を加えた八苦が人たちを苦しめていました。⑤釈迦はこれら八苦から逃れるためにはどうすればよいか悩み、出家しました。⑥釈迦が裕福な王子だったときはもちろんのこと、苦しい修行に耐えていたときも、人生の「苦」は減りませんでした。⑦そうして、快楽に耽るのでも苦行に耐えるのでもない、両極端をさける「中道」を行くのがいいと結論したのです。⑧いまから約2500年前、六年間の苦行を経た釈迦は、インド東部のブッダガヤの菩提樹の下で坐禅を組み、悟りを開きました。⑨坐禅は、仏教ができる前の古代インドの時代から存在した修行の一つです。⑩釈迦が坐禅を組んで悟りを開いたので、仏教に取り入れられるようになりました。

12 The Beginning of Zen, "The Flower Sermon"
花の説話(→拈華微笑)

①One day, the Buddha gathered his disciples to give a lecture as he often would do when he had messages to share with them. ②While the disciples were watching the Buddha, he silently held up a flower. ③Although the disciples tried to capture the meaning of his message, they couldn't find the answer; they were deeply confused.

④However, one of the disciples, *Mahākāśyapa* (摩訶迦葉), gazed at the flower and broke into a smile.

⑤Buddha realized that *Mahākāśyapa* had understood the meaning of his action and he addressed them as follows:

⑥"I possess the true *Dharma* eye (正しい法の目→正法眼蔵), the marvelous mind of *Nirvāna* (涅槃のすばらしいこころ→涅槃妙心), the true form of the formless (本当の形は形をもたない→実相無相), the subtle *Dharma* gate (捉えにくい法門→微妙法門) that does not communicate with words or letters but is a special transmission outside of the scriptures. ⑦This I entrust to *Mahākāśyapa*."

⑧The *Dharma* gate in Buddha's words is thought to be the

34

origin of Zen. ⑨Zen is attaining enlightenment through
起源
meditation and various training.
瞑想　　　　　　　さまざまな修行

12. 禅の始まり「拈華微笑(ねんげみしょう)」

①ある日釈迦は、弟子(でし)たちに伝えたいことがあるときにいつもしていたように、弟子たちを集め、説法をしていました。
②釈迦は弟子たちが見ている前で、無言で花を持ち上げて見せました。
③弟子たちはこのメッセージの意味をつかみとろうとしましたが、答えがわからなくて、とても混乱してしまいました。
④しかし、弟子の一人の摩訶迦葉(まかかしょう)だけが、その花をじっと見つめて微笑(ほほえ)みました。
⑤釈迦には、摩訶迦葉がこの動作の意味を理解したことがわかったので、次のように話しました。
⑥「私には正法眼蔵(しょうぼうげんぞう)、涅槃妙心(ねはんみょうしん)、実相無相(じっそうむそう)、微妙の法門(みみょうのほうもん)がある。微妙の法門とは、言葉や文字では伝えられないものであり(不立文字(ふりゅうもんじ))、経典ではない特別な伝達方法(教外別伝(きょうげべつでん))である。
⑦わたしはこれを摩訶迦葉に託(たく)す」。
⑧釈迦の言葉にある法門が、禅の起源だと考えられています。
⑨禅とは、瞑想(めいそう)やさまざまな修行を通して悟りを得ることです。

13 Zen Was Transmitted from India to China by *Bodhidharma*

①Zen or *Dhyāna* in Sanskrit, a sect of Buddhism, originated in India and spread out across East Asian countries, such as Korea, Japan and Vietnam, through China. ②It is *Bodhidharma* who brought *Dhyāna* from India to China.

③*Bodhidharma* arrived in southern China in 527 after traveling for three years by sea. ④At that time, southern China was dominated by the *Liang* Dynasty. ⑤Emperor *Wu* of *Liang*, a religious and faithful believer, welcomed him. ⑥He asked *Bodhidharma's* opinion about his contribution to Buddhism; *Bodhidharma* answered "no contribution" and denied Emperor *Wu*. ⑦It hurt his feelings.
⑧Not being accepted by Emperor *Wu*, *Bodhidharma* continued to travel to the north and finally arrived at the Northern *Wei* Dynasty. ⑨There, he settled in the *Shaolin*

Monastery, where *Chan* (Chinese translation of Zen) originated.

⑩During the late *Tang* Dynasty (618-907) to the *Song* Dynasty (960-1279), *Chan* was widely accepted by the people, and gradually spread to surrounding countries. ⑪It was the Golden Age of *Chan* in China.

---

13. 禅は達磨大師がインドから中国へ伝えた

①禅は禅定、サンスクリット語でジャーナという仏教の宗派で、インドで発祥し、中国を経て韓国、日本、ベトナムなどのアジア諸国に伝えられました。②禅をインドから中国に伝えたのは、達磨大師です。

③達磨は3年間の船旅の後に、527年、中国の南部にたどり着きました。④当時、中国南部は梁の統治下にありました。⑤信心深い人物であった武帝は、達磨を歓迎しました。⑥彼は達磨に、これまで自分が仏教に対して行なってきた功徳についての意見を求めましたが、達磨はそれは功徳ではないと言って認めませんでした。⑦そのことで、皇帝は気分を害しました。

⑧そのために、武帝に受け入れられなかった達磨は、北に向かって旅を続け、北魏にたどり着きました。⑨そこで少林寺に居を構えますが、そこが禅、中国語でチャンの発祥の地となりました。⑩唐（618-907）の後期から、宋（960-1279）にかけて、禅は広く人々に受け入れられ、しだいに周辺の国に広がりました。⑪この時代が中国での禅の全盛期となります。

14 *Bodhidharma's* Zen

①*Bodhidharma*, whose original name is *Bodhitara*, is known as the father of Zen. ②According to old Chinese documents, he was born as a third prince to the royal family of "*Kang-zhi* land". ③Bodhitara's Buddhist master, *Prajnatara*, was the twenty-seventh patriarch of Indian Buddhism. ⑤Since *Prajnatara* recognized *Bodhitara's* rare talent as a Buddhist, he named his disciple "*Bodhidharma*". ⑥This name embodies the most important word of Buddhism, "*Dharma*".

⑦*Dharma* is a Sanskrit word which means *hou* or the "law of being (universal law of nature)". ⑧*Bodhi*, also a Sanskrit word, means *Satori* or enlightenment. ⑨Thus, his name, *Bodhidharma*, means "get enlightenment of law (perfect knowledge or wisdom)".

⑩*Bodhidharma*, who became the twenty-eighth patriarch of Indian Buddhism, continued to travel around China to

engage in missionary work . ⑪Legend has it that he lived to
布教に従事する　　　　　　　　～という伝説がある
be one hundred fifty.

14. 達磨の禅

①達磨（菩提達磨）は、もとの名を菩提多羅といい、禅の祖師として知られています。②中国の古文書によると、彼は香至国の王室の3番目の王子でした。

④菩提多羅の師、般若多羅はインド仏教の第27番目の祖師でした。⑤般若多羅は、菩提多羅の仏教徒としての才能に気がつき、彼にボディダルマという名をつけました。⑥この名前は仏教で最も重要な語であるダルマ（法）にちなんでつけられました。

⑦ダルマはサンスクリット語で、「存在しているもの」という意味の言葉です。⑧ボディ（菩提）は同じくサンスクリット語で、悟りを意味する言葉です。⑨ですから、菩提達磨という名前は、「法の悟りを得たもの」という意味です。

⑩インド仏教の第28番目の祖師になった菩提達磨は、中国を布教してまわりました。⑪伝説では150歳まで生きたとされています。

15 *Bodhidharma* and *Eka*

① *Bodhidharma* is famous for practicing zazen continuously against a wall in the *Shorin-ji* temple for 9 years. ② *Bodhidharma*'s first acquaintance with *Eka*, his disciple, is very impressive. ③ *Eka*, who was eager to be a disciple of *Bodhidharma*, visited the *Shorin-ji* temple. ④ *Bodhidharma* would not admit him, even though *Eka* remained standing in waist deep snow for a long time. ⑤ Then *Eka* cut off his left arm to show his resolution. ⑥ Consequently, he was admitted to be a disciple of *Bodhidharma*, and became a second master.

⑦ There is a dialogue between them known as "*Bodhidharma* Pacifies Heart-mind".

⑧ *Eka*: I need your help to calm this uneasy heart of mine.

⑨ *Bodhidharma*: I can do it if you take out your heart and bring it to me.

⑩ *Eka*: I tried to do it but I couldn't.

⑪*Bodhidharma*: Now your heart is constant.
　　　　　　　　　　　　　　　　　　安定した
⑫Taking out your heart is a metaphor for understanding the
　　　　　　　　　　　　　　比喩
condition of your heart. ⑬It is important to see your true
状態
mind. ⑭This story demonstrates the essence of Zen.
　　　　　　　　　　　～を説明する　　真髄(本質)

---

15. 達磨と慧可(えか)

①達磨は、少林寺の壁に向かって9年間坐禅を組んだという伝説で有名です。②その達磨と弟子の慧可の出会いのエピソードは強烈です。③達磨に入門することを望んだ慧可は、少林寺を訪れます。④慧可は、腰まで埋め尽くす雪の中で、達磨に入門を懇願(こんがん)しましたが、達磨は慧可の入門を認めませんでした。⑤慧可は自分の左腕を切り落として覚悟の意思を見せました。⑥こうして慧可は入門を許され、第二祖になりました。
⑦彼らの問答に有名な「達磨安心」があります。
⑧慧可:「不安な心を安定させてほしいのです」
⑨達磨:「心を取り出して持ってきたら安定させよう」
⑩慧可:「心を取り出そうとしましたが取り出せませんでした」
⑪達磨:「おまえの心はもう安定した」
⑫不安な心を取り出してみるというのは、不安に思う自分の心の状態を知るということの比喩(ひゆ)です。⑬自分の本当の心を知ることが大切です。⑭この話は禅の真髄(しんずい)をあらわしています。

16 　*Enō's Zen*

①*Enō*, the sixth master of Chinese Zen, was poor and not a well educated man, who supported *Gunin*, a master descended from the fifth generation founder of Chinese Zen, as a servant. ②When *Gunin* selected his successor, he confronted *Enō* and *Jinshū*, an excellent disciple. ③*Gunin* had them write poetry to express the mind of enlightenment.
④*Jinshū* wrote: The mind of enlightenment is like a mirror.

⑤Priests always train so that the mirror does not become cloudy.

⑥*Enō* expressed: The human is naturally pure. ⑦The mirror never becomes cloudy.

⑧What *Enō's* poetry means is that the mind is naturally innocent, and this represents a distinction of Zen. ⑨*Gunin*, evaluating *Enō*, selected him as the successor.

⑩*Enō* became a sixth patriarch in southern area and developed Chinese Zen with an idea that "the enlightenment

is in the daily life". ⑪*Jinshū*, who had lost the competition
　　　　　　　　　　　　　　　　　～に敗れる　競争
with *Enō*, was engaged in missionary work of Indian style
　　　　　～に従事する　伝道
Zen in the northern area. ⑫His sect decreased as the *Tang*
　　　　　　　　　　　　　宗派　縮小した
Dynasty declined, because he had a strong relationship
　　　　　衰退した　　　　　　　　　　　　　　　関係
with the government authorities.
　　　政治の権力者

---

16. 慧能(えのう)の禅

①達磨から数えて六代目の慧能は、貧しく学問がない人で、中国禅宗の第五祖、弘忍(ぐにん)のもとで下働きをしていました。②弘忍は後継者を選ぶときに、慧能と、優秀な弟子である神秀(じんしゅう)を対決させました。③二人に、それぞれ悟りの心境をつづった詩を書かせたのです。

④神秀は「悟った心は鏡のようなものだ。⑤ゴミがつかないように常に修行するのだ」と書きました。

⑥慧能は「人間は本来清浄(せいじょう)である（本来無一物(ほんらいむいちもつ)）。⑦鏡は曇(くも)らない」と表現しました。⑧もともと心には囚(とら)われるものなど何もないという慧能の詩は、禅の特徴をよく表しています。⑨弘忍は慧能を評価し、神秀を抑えて抜擢(ばってき)しました。

⑩慧能は南部で第六祖になり、中国禅を発展させ、「日常生活に悟りがある」という考えで弟子を育成し大きく発展しました。
⑪負けた神秀は北部でインド的な禅を実践しました。⑫権力者と深く関わったため、唐の衰退とともに縮小していきました。

17 *Baso* and *Hyakujō*

①*Nangaku Ejō*, a disciple of *Enō*, and *Baso Dōitsu*, a disciple of Ejō made the attitude for zazen clear. ②They concluded that the aim of practicing zazen was not to attain enlightenment but the action of zazen itself was significant.
③*Baso* mentioned that the "mind of Buddha" was not outside of oneself but it was the mind that existed in oneself. ④The idea was widely accepted.
⑤*Hyakujō Ekai*, a disciple of *Baso* is known for the saying: "One day not work, one day not eat". ⑥Indian Buddhism forbade labor by the priests. ⑦Since the current social circumstances prevented priests from receiving offerings from the people at the time in China, *Hyakujō* set an example to work. ⑧He showed that the most important training is labor. ⑨He is said to be the priest who reformed the Zen sect and made regulations for it.
⑩After that time, in ninth century China, Buddhism began

to be oppressed. ⑪Even in this situation, Zen was widely
spread in spite of the oppression, because Zen did not rely
upon the sutra but set the daily life as the place of the
training.

17. 馬祖と百丈

①慧能の弟子の南岳懐譲とその弟子の馬祖道一によって坐禅に対する姿勢が明確化されました。②坐禅を組んだ結果、悟りが得られるのではなく、ただ坐禅をすることに意味があるとしました。

③馬祖は、仏心は自分の外にあるのではなく、もともと自分の内にある心そのものなのだと説きました（即心即仏）。④その考えは広く受け入れられました。

⑤馬祖の弟子の百丈懐海は、「一日作さざれば一日食らわず」という言葉で有名です。⑥インド仏教は、出家者の労働を禁止していました。⑦中国では、当時お布施などを得にくい社会状況だったので、百丈が率先して労働を勧めました。⑧労働こそが、一番大切な修行であるとしたのです。⑨戒律の改革をし、禅宗の規則を作った人といわれています。

⑩その後、9世紀に中国では、仏教が弾圧されるようになりました。⑪そんな中、禅宗は経典に頼らず、日常生活を修行の場にしていたために、弾圧をものともせずに広く定着したのです。

18 Zen in Japan ①

①In the *Asuka* period, Zen had already been introduced to Japan from China. ②Practically speaking, the spread of Zen was full blown during the *Kamakura* period. ③*Eisai*, a priest of the *Tendai* school, traveled to China during the *Song* Dynasty, received certification, and established the *Rinzai* school. ④30 years after *Eisai*, *Dōgen*, also a priest of the *Tendai* school, went to China during the *Song* Dynasty, received certification from the *Sōtō* school, and established a temple in *Kyōto*. ⑤At that time, the Mongolians, taking advantage of the decline of the *Song* Dynasty, invaded China and established the *Yuan* Dynasty, which dominated China. ⑥Under the domination of the Mongolians, Chinese Zen declined and eminent priests immigrated to Japan. ⑦Particularly active among them were *Rankei Dōryu*, who brought several styles of Chinese Zen, and *Mugaku Sōgen*, who spiritually supported the *Kamakura* Shogunate when the *Yuan*

Dynasty attacked Japan.

⑧Because *samurais* accepted Zen as practical teaching, the center of Zen moved to *Kamakura* as the *Kamakura* Shogunate prospered. ⑨Most of the priests in this period doubled both as Zen priests and as priests of other schools such as the *Shingon* school and the *Tendai* school.

---

18. 日本の禅①

①禅は、日本にはすでに飛鳥時代に中国から伝わっていました。②実際、禅が本格的に広がったのは、鎌倉時代になってからです。③天台宗の僧侶だった栄西が、中国の宋に入り印可を受け、日本で臨済宗を始めました。④その約30年後、同じく天台僧だった道元が、宋に渡り曹洞宗の印可を受けて京都で布教活動を始めました。

⑤この頃、中国では宋の衰退につけ込んでモンゴル人が攻め入り、元王朝が支配するようになりました。⑥モンゴルの支配により、禅宗は衰退の一途をたどり、中国禅の高僧たちが次々に日本に渡来しました。⑦中国禅の厳しい修行を伝えた蘭渓道隆と、元が日本に襲来したときに鎌倉幕府の精神的支えとなった無学祖元が活躍しました。

⑧禅宗の実践的な教えが武士の間で受け入れられたので、禅宗の拠点は、鎌倉幕府の繁栄とともに鎌倉に移りました。⑨鎌倉時代の禅僧の多くは、真言宗や天台宗の僧を兼ねていました。

19 Zen in Japan ②

①In the *Muromachi* period, the Shogunate family, *Ashikaga*, protected the Zen schools. ②*Kyōto's* Five Zen temples were known as "*Kyōto's* Five Mountains", and the five temples in *Kamakura* as "*Kamakura's* Five Mountains". ③Among these ten temples, the shogunate designated the *Nanzen-ji* temple as the leader, and all the temples were managed from there. ④*Musō Soseki*, a priest known as an eminent garden designer, appeared on the scene and contributed to the culture of Zen Buddhism.
⑤As time passed, and as the country came under civil disorder, Zen spread to the people. ⑥In the Age of Civil Wars, top *samurai*s such as *Oda Nobunaga* and *Takeda Shingen* tried to train themselves even as they were struggling under circumstances near death. ⑦In the *Edo* period, the *Rinzai* school was reformed by *Hakuin*, who lead people to Zen. ⑧He systemized Zen with *kōans* and

educated many disciples; as a result Japanese Zen was now complete. ⑨In the *Meiji* period, the new government decided to make *Shintō* a national religion, and Buddhism was oppressed. ⑩After this period of oppression, *Suzuki Daisetsu*, a scholar of Zen, introduced Zen positively outside of Japan, and Japanese Zen was spread to the world.

19. 日本の禅②

①室町時代になって、将軍家である足利家は禅宗を保護しました。②京都の五つの禅寺は京都五山、鎌倉の五つの禅寺は鎌倉五山として知られています。③両五山の上に南禅寺を置き、すべて幕府が管理しました。④庭つくりでも有名な天龍寺の禅僧・夢窓疎石が現れ、禅が文化面に大きく貢献しました。

⑤やがて国が乱れるとともに、禅は民衆にも広がっていきました。⑥戦国時代になると、織田信長や武田信玄などの武将たちは、常に死と背中合わせの過酷な日常の中、禅によって自らを鍛えようとしました。⑦江戸時代に入り、衰退していた臨済宗が白隠によって復興し、一般の民衆に禅が広がりました。⑧白隠は公案を体系化し、たくさんの弟子を育成し、日本人のための禅が完成しました。

⑨明治時代、新政府は神道を国の宗教とし、仏教を弾圧しました。⑩国内では受難が続きましたが、禅の研究者、鈴木大拙が海外に向け積極的に紹介し、日本の禅は世界に広がりました。

20 Three Zen Schools

①In the *Rinzai* school, to attain enlightenment, followers would consider "*Kōans*" given by their master while sitting zazen. ②When they have reflected and come to a conclusion, they go to the master's room and ask them to judge it. ③Zen using "*Kōans*" which is called "*Kōan* Zen", had been supported by the aristocracy and the senior *samurais*.

④The character of the *Sōtō* school is symbolized by the phrases, "the Orthodox *Dharma*" and "focusing only on just sitting". ⑤"Orthodox" means to share the teachings just as *Gautama Siddhārtha* did. ⑥This school was accepted by the *samurais* and local farmers with the basic idea that "to sit" is the only way to attain enlightenment.

⑦In the beginning of the *Edo* period, *Ingen*, who was a Chinese priest, founded the *Ōbaku* school at the *Manpuku-ji* temple located in *Uji*, *Kyōto*. ⑧The Zen introduced by *In-*

gen from China of the *Ming* Dynasty was very different from the Zen founded in Japan. ⑨The priests read their Buddhist texts in Chinese. ⑩The style of the temple and the statue of Buddha were executed with Chinese characteristics. ⑪This difference shook the Buddhist community.

---

20. 三つの禅宗

①臨済宗は、坐禅をしながら、師から出される「公案」を考えることで悟りを開く宗派です。②与えられた公案を工夫して、自分なりの見解が出たとき、師の部屋へ行き、答え合わせをしてもらいます。③この公案を用いて悟る「公案禅」は、主に貴族や上流武士に支持されました。

④曹洞宗の特徴は、道元が提唱する「正伝の仏法」と「只管打坐」に象徴されます。⑤正伝とは、釈迦から伝えられた教えを、そのまま伝えるということです。⑥この宗派は、ひたすら坐禅をすることが悟りを開く道であるということで、地方の武士や農民に受け入れられました。

⑦黄檗宗は、江戸時代初期、京都宇治の萬福寺において、中国人の隠元によって開かれました。⑧隠元がもたらした明の時代の禅は、それまでの日本の禅とは大きく異なりました。⑨読経は、古い中国式の発音で行なわれました。⑩寺院や仏像の様式もすべて中国ふうでした。⑪その違いは、江戸の仏教界に揺さぶりを与えたのです。

People Influenced by Zen / 禅の影響を受けた人々 ①

Matsuo Bashō 松尾芭蕉

Matsuo Bashō, born to a lower *samurai's* family in *Iga Ueno*, gave up his title and went to *Edo*. There, he joined the *Danrin* sect, a *haiku* group known for its liberal and eccentric style. At the age of thirty-seven, disillusioned with the way that *haiku* was being used: as a competition for comedy and humor; he moved to *Fukagawa* from *Nihonbashi*, which was considered the center for *haiku*. At this time he met Master *Buchō* of *Kashima Konponji* temple. His *haiku*, influenced by Zen Buddhism, had been changing to a style in which he focused on observing an object and then expressing the nature of the object, in a simple way. His style, influenced by Zen, is called *Shōfu*. He wrote many *haikus* in this style which embodied "*wabi*" and "*sabi*", both intrinsic to Japanese aesthetic values. One of the most popular *haikus*, "An old pond, a frog jumps into, sound of water" was inspired by a conversation between Master *Buchō* and *Bashō*.

伊賀上野の下級武士の家に生まれた松尾芭蕉は、身分を捨てて江戸に出ました。江戸では、奇抜で自由な誹風で知られる談林派に属しました。37歳のころ、滑稽と華やかさを競う当時の俳壇を嫌い、俳壇の中心であった日本橋から深川に転居。草庵で暮らすようになりました。芭蕉が鹿島根本寺の仏頂禅師に出会ったのはこのころです。禅の影響を受けた芭蕉の句は、無心に対象を観察し、簡素に本質を表現する作風に変化していきました。禅の影響を受けた芭蕉の作風は蕉風と呼ばれ、日本の美意識の原点ともいえる「わび」・「さび」を体現した多くの作品を残しました。仏頂禅師との禅問答によって導かれたといわれる「古池や蛙飛び込む水の音」の句は、たいへん親しまれています。

Chapter 3

Zen's Practices

第3章
禅の修行

Zen Buddhism

21 What is Zen Training?

①Zen is not a thing to think about but is training. ②You can not attain enlightenment even if you read many books and study hard. ③Enlightenment could be explained as having the same mental condition as the Buddha had when he attained enlightenment under the *Bodhi* Tree.
④Enlightenment can be attained when you clean up your mind which is ordinarily messy. ⑤Zen training strips away fixed ideas and prejudices and reorganizes the mind.
⑥Now I quote one story. ⑦In the *Meiji* period, one scholar visited the *Hakusan* training hall in *Tokyo* to see the Old Master *Nan-in*. ⑧*Nan-in*, listening to the scholar, poured tea into a cup. ⑨He continued to pour even after the cup was full. ⑩The scholar said: "Master! The tea is overflowing."
⑪The master answered: "Yes. It is similar to you. ⑫Your mind is filled with study, and there is no room for what I

tell you ." ⑬This story explains Zen very well.

21. 禅の修行とは

①禅とは理屈ではなく、ただ修行を実践するのみです。②本を読んで研究したからといって悟りが得られるものではありません。③悟りとは、「釈迦が菩提樹の木の下で経験した精神状態になること」といえるでしょう。

④悟りとは、雑然とした頭の中を空っぽにすることです。⑤固定観念や先入観を取り除き、心を整理することが、禅の修行です。

⑥こんな話があります。⑦明治時代、東京の白山道場の南隠老師のもとに一人の学者が尋ねてきました。⑧老師は学者の話を聞きながら、急須でお茶を注ぎました。⑨老師は茶碗がいっぱいになってもまだ注いでいました。⑩そのため、「老師、お茶があふれています」と学者が言いました。⑪南隠老師は、「そうだ。あんたと同じだ。⑫学問が頭にいっぱい詰まっているから、わしが何を言っても入る余地はないだろう」と答えたそうです。⑬これは、わかりやすいたとえ話です。

22 How to Become a Priest

①While Zen temples are traditionally handed down from father to son, others can also become priests. ②In the old days, children began Zen training as a servant in a temple. ③Nowadays, anyone who wants to become a priest, usually begins learning in an academy of Buddhism.
④However, one can become apprenticed to a master, and learn Buddhism from the master of the temple.

⑤Upon graduating from the academy or finishing basic studies in the temple, they participate in a ceremony called "*tokudo*". ⑥This ceremony, held in the head temple, functions to separate students from the world and the way of Buddhism, when they shave their head and, from this time, wear the black robes of the priest. ⑦Following the *tokudo*, they enter the monastery and train as *unsui* or trainees. ⑧After three years of training, they are certificated to be a master. ⑨They can expand the period of training, if they feel it has not been enough. ⑩In the monastery, all the priests are treated equally. ⑪They do not need any expenses for living there.

平等に扱われる
経費

22. 僧として修行するには

①僧侶になるのは、寺の跡取りだけとは限らなく、それ以外の人でもなることができます。②昔は、寺の小僧として寺での生活をして修行を始めました。③最近では、僧侶を目指す人のほとんどは、仏教専門の学校に入って仏教を学ぶことからスタートします。

④学校へ行かなくても、和尚を探して、弟子入りし、一定の期間、寺で修行して仏教を学ぶこともできます。

⑤仏教の学校を卒業した人や、寺の見習いをしていた人の次のステップが、僧侶となるための出家の儀式である「得度」です。⑥これは、世俗の生活を捨て、剃髪染衣して仏道に専心するための儀式で、本山で行なわれます。⑦得度した人は僧堂へ入門し、雲水として修行を積みます。⑧3年間修行すると、住職の資格がもらえます。⑨まだ修行が足りないと感じたら、この期間を延ばすこともできます。⑩僧堂では、どの修行僧もみな平等に扱われます。⑪生活のためのお金はかかりません。

23 Before Entering the Monastery

①A priest in training is called *unsui*, which means clouds and water in Japanese. ②It is a metaphor for the priests who travel and visit various masters to learn the Buddhist teachings, and are like clouds and water.

③*Unsuis* are training under masters in monasteries in each of the Zen Buddhist schools all over the country.

④A newcomer, having straightened his robes, goes onto the temple grounds. ⑤He bows at the porch step and shouts out "Please!" in a loud voice. ⑥When an *unsui* of the monastery comes out saying "How?" the newcomer tells him his name and gives him his application and personal history. ⑦The *unsui* of the monastery tells the newcomer; "This monastery is full. Please go back." ⑧Then he goes inside and doesn't come out again. ⑨The newcomer sits on the step, lowers his head, and continues to beg to be accepted. ⑩He is being tested on his determination to train himself. ⑪When evening

comes, he is allowed to take a rest in a small room by the
porch. ⑫In the morning, he goes back to the porch again, lowers his head, and continues to beg. ⑬After begging for three days, only then, after practicing zazen while facing the wall for five days, if he passes all these trials, is he finally permitted to "enter the gate".

23. 僧堂に入門するまで

①禅宗では、修行僧のことを雲水と呼びますが、これは雲と水を表します。②さまざまな師を訪ね、仏道を求める修行僧のことを、定まることのない雲や水にたとえたものです。③禅宗の各派は全国に僧堂を持ち、老師のもとで雲水が修行をしています。
④装束を調えた新参者は、僧堂がある本山の境内に入ります。⑤玄関の式台に腰をかけ、頭を下げ、「たのみましょー」と大声で呼びます。⑥中から「どーれ」と現れた雲水に、名前を名乗り、願書や履歴書などを渡します。⑦受け取った雲水は「満員なのでお引きとりください」と言います。⑧そして、奥へ下がってもう姿を見せません。⑨新参者は玄関の式台で、頭を下げたまま懇願し続けます。⑩修行に対する決心の強さを試されます。⑪夕方は投宿といって、玄関脇にある小部屋でやすむことが許されます。⑫朝になると、また玄関で頭を下げ、懇願し続けます。⑬3日間の懇願が終わり、その後5日間の壁に向かっての坐禅の修行を通った者だけが、入門を許されます。

24 Training Life of Unsui

①Each of the *unsuis* who are accepted in the monastery, are given a small space the size of a tatami mat, called a "*tan*" or a "single". ②In this space, they practice zazen, take their meals and sleep at night.

③Everything the *unsuis* do, are determined in detail by rules. ④For example, at the *Rinzai* school, the *unsuis* are awaken at three o'clock in the morning by the ringing of a hand bell. ⑤They read the sutras, practice zazen, have a breakfast of rice porridge, clean the monastery, and labor until eleven thirty according to the set schedule. ⑥After reading the sutras again, they eat lunch, and complete the afternoon routine. ⑦After supper, they read the sutras for the evening, and go to bed at nine o'clock. ⑧All of these tasks are begun with different signals, such as the sound of bells, drums or beating on a board. ⑨All the actions of *unsuis'* daily

第3章 禅の修行

life, such as the way to hold chopsticks and a bowl, or
to take off the sandals, are regulated under the law
called "*Kiku*" or "the code of conduct". ⑩All the tasks
of *unsuis* are components of training. (see pp.62-63)

24. 雲水の修行生活

①入門を許された雲水は、僧堂の両側にある「単」と呼ばれる畳を敷いた1畳分のスペースが与えられます。②そこは、坐禅を組んだり、食事をとったり、夜は眠る場所になります。
③一日の行動は、すべて事細かに決められています。④たとえば、臨済宗の寺では、真夜中ともいえる午前3時半に振鈴と呼ばれる鈴の音で起床。⑤朝の読経の後、坐禅、朝の食事、掃除の作務が一連のスケジュールとして11時半まで続きます。⑥日中の読経の後、昼の食事、午後の作務をします。⑦夜の食事と坐禅を終え、9時に就寝するという一日です。
⑧この一連の修行は、鐘、太鼓、板などを叩くことが合図になって始められます。⑨雲水たちは、箸や小鉢の持ち方、草履の脱ぎ方などの日常生活のすべての動作を「規矩」という規則で細かく定められています。⑩日常のどの行為も修行なのです（p62〜63参照）。

入門する雲水（曹洞宗の場合）

Procedure for the Unsui to Enter the Monastery (The *Sōtō* School Style)

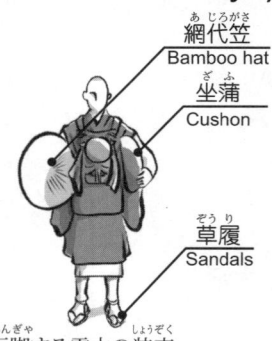

網代笠（あじろがさ）
Bamboo hat

坐蒲（ざふ）
Cushion

草履（ぞうり）
Sandals

行脚（あんぎゃ）する雲水の装束（しょうぞく）。

The travel costume of the *unsui*.

山門（さんもん）について拝礼（はいれい）する雲水。

The *unsui* sits and bows down at the gate of the monastery.

行動の合図になる「鳴（な）らし物」

Sounds Used to Signal the Beginning of Routines.

【版木（はんぎ）】行動の合図。
【Woodcut(*Hangi*)】 Signal for beginning new tasks.

【雲版（うんぱん）】食事の合図。
【Cloud board(*Unban*)】 Signal for mealtime.

【振鈴（しんれい）】起床を知らせる。
【Hand bell(*Shinrei*)】 Signal for rising.

雲水のスペースの「単」

"Single" or "Tan", the Personal Space of the Unsui.

単は一人分が畳一枚の広さで奥の棚に布団や食器が入る。

The *tan* is an area with a closet where *unsui* puts bedding and tableware. Each *unsui* is allowed one tatami sized area.

雲水は単で坐禅を組み、食事をとり、眠る。

The *tan* is where *unsuis* practice zazen, have meals and sleep.

雲水の「作務」

Routine of the Unsui, *Samu*

作務とは、日常生活に必要なさまざまな作業。中でももっとも重要なのは掃除だ。

Samu is the various work routines in the daily life of an *unsui*. The most important among them is sweeping.

25 Manner of Zazen in Monastery

①The important things in practicing zazen is to straighten up, control the breathing and control the mind. ②In the temple, you practice zazen on a *tan*.

③The manner is different between the *Sōtō* school and the *Rinzai* school. ④In the monastery of the *Rinzai* school, you put your palms together, and walk toward a tan. ⑤Before getting on the tan, you lower your head and put your palms together; then you turn to your right, facing your back to the *tan*, finally you lower your head and put your palms together again. ⑥Using your leg in a backward movement, you climb backward up onto the *tan*, being careful not to touch the edge of the *tan* with your foot; and sit down on a cushion with your back against the wall. ⑦After sitting on the *tan*, you straighten your sandals and take a position of zazen.
⑧In the monastery of the *Sōtō* school, after you make a fist with your right hand, cover it with the left hand, and then place them on your chest; you walk toward a *tan*. ⑨When you reach the *tan*, you

put your palms together, and lower your head. ⑩Then, you turn to the right and <u>put your back to</u> the tan, pulling a cushion or *zafu* behind you, before you sit down on it. ⑪Now, you <u>lift your legs up</u> quickly onto the tan, being careful not to touch the edge of tan with your body and straighten your sandals. ⑫After sitting on the tan, you turn to the right and face the wall, then you take a position of zazen.

~に背中を向ける / 坐蒲 / ~する前に / ~を持ち上げる

---

25. 僧堂における坐禅の作法

①坐禅では正しい姿勢をし（調身）、呼吸を調え（調息）、心のありようを調える（調心）のが大事だとされています。②禅寺では、「単」にあがり、坐禅を組みます。

③坐禅の作法は、臨済宗と曹洞宗で違います。④臨済宗の寺の場合は、単に向かって合掌しながら歩きます。⑤単の前で、合掌低頭し、右回りでまわり、後ろ向きになって再び合掌低頭します。⑥右足を後ろに持ち上げ、縁に足をかけないようにあがり、壁を背にして座布団に坐ります。⑦履物をそろえ、坐禅の姿勢をとります。

⑧曹洞宗の寺の場合、握った右手を左手で覆い、胸にあてる動作（叉手）をしながら単に向かいます。⑨単の前で合掌低頭し、右回りで単に背を向けます。⑩単の縁に体が触れないように、後ろ手で坐蒲と呼ばれるクッションを引き寄せ、腰を下ろします。⑪両足が縁に触れないように単にあがり、履物をそろえます。⑫右回りにまわり、壁に向かい、坐禅の姿勢をとります。

26　　　　How to Do Zazen

①There are two ways of sitting: the full-lotus position and the half-lotus position. ②The full-lotus position is sitting down, legs crossed, with the soles of your feet upward. ③Sit down, with your legs crossed, on a cushion folded to lift up your hips. ④Arrange the right foot on your left thigh and left foot on your right thigh. ⑤Position both feet so the soles are upward and both knees touch the floor.

⑥In the half-lotus position, only the sole of the left foot is upward and both knees are arranged in a way to touch the floor. ⑦It's ideal that the tips of the toes, are outside of the thighs, and with the knees and the coccyx, form an isosceles triangle.

⑧As for the hands, put your right hand on your left leg with the palm facing upward and put the left hand on it, palms together. ⑨Align both thumbs together and it will

66

form an oval. ⑩Then put the hands on the spot called the
"*tanden*," below the navel. ⑪The easiest way for the
beginner is to wrap the fingers of the right hand around
the thumb of the left hand. (see pp.68-69)

26. 坐禅の組み方

①足の組み方には「結跏趺坐」と「半跏趺坐」があります。
②結跏趺坐とは両足の裏を上に向けて組む坐り方です。③座布団を二つ折りしたものに浅く腰掛け、あぐらをかきます。④右の足を左の腿の上に置き、左足は右の腿の上に置きます。⑤両足の裏が上を向き、両方の膝が床についているようにします。
⑥半跏趺坐では、左足の裏だけ上に向くようにして、両膝は床につけます。
⑦足の指先が太腿の外側から出ていて、両膝と尾てい骨が正三角形になっていれば理想的です。
⑧手は、右手の掌を上にして左足の上に置き、左手の掌を乗せて重ねます。⑨親指同士を触れ合わせて楕円形をつくります。
⑩手がヘソの下の丹田という場所に位置するようにおきます。
⑪初心者は、左手の親指を右手の5本の指で包むように握り、左手の残りの指で右手の指を覆うやり方があります（p68～69参照）。

合掌・叉手・低頭
Praying Hands, Forked Hands, Lowering the Head.

合掌 Praying Hands

指先を鼻の高さに上げ、手は胸から少し離す。
Keep your fingertip at the level of the nose and keep your hands away from the chest.

叉手 Forked Hands

左手を親指を内にして握り、右手で覆う。
Arrange the palm of your right hand facing upward and put the left hand on it.

低頭 Bowing Low

膝を伸ばして腰から曲げ、深く頭を下げる。
Stretch your knees, bend at the waist, and lower your head.

臨済宗と曹洞宗の坐禅
Zazen of the Rinzai School and the Sōtō School.

臨済宗の坐禅
Zazen of the Rinzai School

壁を背にして坐る。
Sit with your back against the wall.

曹洞宗の坐禅
Zazen of the Sōtō School

壁に向かって坐る。
Sit facing the wall.

坐禅における足の組み方

The Cross-legged Position of Zazen.

結跏趺坐 Full-lotus Position

半跏趺坐 Half-lotus Position

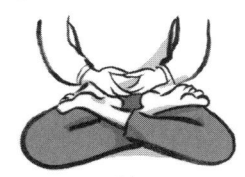

右の足を左の腿の上に置き、左足は右の腿の上に置く。両足の裏が上を向くようにする。

Arrange the right foot on your left thigh and left foot on your right thigh so that the soles of both feet are upward.

左足の裏だけ上に向くようにして、両膝は床につける。

Only the sole of the left foot is upward and both knees are arranged in a way to touch the floor.

坐禅における手の置き方

Positions of the Hands for Zazen.

正式の形
Formal Position

初心者向けの形
Position for Beginners

両方の親指を一直線にして、楕円形をつくる。

Align both thumbs together and it will form an oval.

左手の親指を右手の5本の指で包むように握り、左手の残りの指で右手の指を覆う。

Wrap around the thumb of the left hand with the fingers of the right hand.

27. The Posture of Zazen and Breathing
姿勢

①After crossing your legs and hands, <u>straighten your body</u>.
姿勢を正しく整える

②Then relax and move your <u>upper body</u> to the right and left to find a <u>stable position</u>.
上半身　左右に　安定した位置

③Also move your body <u>back and forth</u> to <u>vertically align</u> your body.
前後に　垂直にそろえる(→垂直になる)　アライン

④You straighten your <u>backbone</u>, <u>draw in</u> your <u>chin</u> and <u>focus on</u> the *tanden*, a point <u>located below</u> your <u>navel</u>.
背骨　～をひく　～に集中する　丹田　～の下に　ヘソ

⑤Your head and <u>knees</u> should <u>form</u> an <u>isosceles triangle</u> as seen <u>from the front</u>.
膝　～の形をつくる　二等辺三角形　正面から

⑥<u>As for</u> your <u>eye level</u>, you look straight <u>ahead</u> then <u>drop</u> your eyes <u>at a forty-five degree angle</u> to look one meter ahead.
～については　目の高さ(→視線)　下げる　45度の角度で　先

⑦Not looking at <u>something specific</u> but looking <u>generally</u>.
特定の何か　あまねく

⑧Do not be <u>busy looking around</u>.
せわしなくあたりを見渡す(→キョロキョロする)

⑨Close your mouth softly, <u>inhale</u> through the nose, and <u>exhale</u> slowly through a small opening in the mouth.
吸い込む　吐き出す

⑩At that moment, <u>concentrate on</u> the *tanden*.
～に集中する

⑪As you

breathe in, be aware that the air circulates through your
body. ⑫It is effective to clear your mind of unnecessary
thoughts by counting in your head while breathing.
(see pp.74-75)

27. 姿勢の調え方と呼吸法

①足と手を組んだところで、姿勢を正しく調えます。
②力を抜いて、上半身を左右に振り子のように揺さぶり、安定する位置を決めます。③前後にも揺さぶり、垂直になるようにします。④背骨をまっすぐ伸ばし、あごをひき、重心をヘソの下の丹田に集中させます。⑤正面からみて、頭と膝の先できれいな二等辺三角形ができるようにします。

⑥視線は、正面を見て角度を下げ、1メートル先の45度斜め下を見ます。⑦特定のものを見るのではなく、視界を広くします。⑧キョロキョロしてはいけません。

⑨口は軽く閉じて、呼吸は鼻から吸い込んで、細く開いた口からできるだけ長く息を吐ききります（腹式呼吸）。⑩そのとき、意識を丹田に集中させます。⑪息を吸い込むとき、身体の中を吸い込んだ息が巡るように意識します。⑫心の中で数をかぞえて呼吸する方法（数息観）は、雑念を払うのに効果があります（p74-75参照）。

28 How to Be Hit with Keisaku and Finish Zazen

①When you hear the word 'zazen', you may have images
                                                  イメージ
of the sight of a trainee who is hit by a priest with a
   風景   修行者
wooden stick. ②The stick which the priest is carrying is
木製の棒
called '*keisaku*'.

③It is not a punishment to be hit with a *keisaku*. ④It is for
              罰
stimulating you when you have lost concentration or
~に刺激を与える   集中力
posture. ⑤You can ask to be hit with the *keisaku* when
姿勢
you feel sleepy or are losing concentration. ⑥To place
        眠気
your palms together, is a sign that you require *keisaku*.
手のひらを合わせること(→合掌) 合図   ~を求める
⑦The way in which you are hit by the *keisaku* is different
in the *Rinzai* school than from the *Sōtō* school. ⑧In the
Rinzai school, you are hit twice on both shoulders from a
                                          肩
priest standing in front of you. ⑨In the *Sōtō* school, you
will be hit on the right shoulder from a priest behind you.
⑩In both cases, you are hit after lowering your head,
  どちらの場合も   頭を下げる

72

placing your palms together and bowing.
⑪When you finish zazen, release your hands, place your palms together, and bow slightly. ⑫Then you put your hands on your knees, palms facing upward, and swing your body from side to side. ⑬Finally, you stand up slowly, and place your palms together. (see p.75)

28. 警策の受け方と坐禅の終え方

①坐禅といえば、僧に木の棒で叩かれている風景が思い浮かぶでしょう。②僧が持ち歩いている棒は警策と呼ばれています。③警策で打つのは、罰としてではありません。④修行者が集中を欠いていたり、姿勢が乱れてきたりしたときに、刺激を与えて気を引き締めるために打ちます。⑤坐禅中に眠気に襲われたときや、散漫になったときは、自分から警策を求めることもできます。⑥合掌することが、警策を求める合図です。

⑦警策を受ける作法は臨済宗と曹洞宗で異なります。⑧臨済宗は、正面から両肩を2回、警策を受けます。⑨曹洞宗では、背後から警策を右肩に受けます。⑩どちらも頭を低くして受け、終わったら合掌低頭をします。

⑪坐禅を終えるときは、手を解き、合掌し、頭を下げます。⑫掌を上に向け、膝に置き、身体を左右に揺らします。⑬足を解いてゆっくりと立ち上がり、最後に合掌します。(p.75参照)

姿勢の調え方

How to Arrange the Posture

あごをひく
Draw in your chin

背筋はまっすぐ
Straighten your back

丹田に集中
Concentrate on the *tanden*

力を抜き、上半身を左右に揺さぶり、安定する位置を決める。前後にも揺さぶり垂直にする。

Relax and move your upper body to the right and left to find a stable position. Also move your body back and forth to vertically align your body.

視線の置き方

How to Fix the Eye Level

斜め下を見る
Look downward

45°

1m

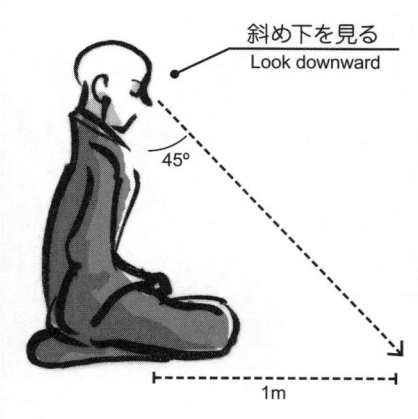

1メートル先の45度斜め下を見る。特定のものを見るのではなく、広い範囲を見る。

Drop your eyes at a forty-five degree angle to look one meter ahead. Not looking at something specific but looking generally.

呼吸法

How to Breath

呼吸は鼻から吸い込んで、細く開いた口からできるだけ長く息を吐ききる。意識を丹田に集中する。

Close your mouth softly, inhale through the nose, and exhale slowly through a small opening in the mouth. At that moment, concentrate on the *tanden*.

丹田
tanden

警策の受け方

How to Be Hit with Keisaku

臨済宗
The *Rinzai* School

正面から両肩を２回、警策を受ける。

You are hit twice on both shoulders from a priest standing in front of you.

曹洞宗
The *Sōtō* School

背後から警策を右肩に受ける。

You will be hit on the right shoulder from a priest behind you.

29 Reciting Sutras

①In Zen schools of Buddhism, priests seek to learn the truth, which can not be described with words, through zazen training. ②However, they do not neglect to recite the sutras. ③In Zen temples, priests recite the sutras as part of their routine before the morning and evening labors as well as before meals.

④The sutras usually recited, are "*Shigu Seigan*" or "The Four *Bodhisattva* Vows" and "*Hannya Shingyo*" or "The Heart Sutra".

⑤The Four *Bodhisattva* Vows contain four vows: saving all creatures in the world, abandoning all infinite desires, learning all the infinite teachings of Buddhism, and being sure to become a Buddha even though the way is infinitely long.

⑥The Heart Sutra is one which is the most familiar to Japanese people even to those outside of the temple. ⑦The

第3章 禅の修行

one which is usually recited in Japan was translated from
(〜から翻訳された)
Sanskrit into Chinese by Master *Genjo* of the *Tang*
(サンスクリット語)　　　　　　　　　　　　　　　(玄奘)
Dynasty.

⑧It is said that all the teachings of the Buddha are included
(含む)
in the short text of 262 Chinese characters.
(漢字)

---

29. 読経(どきょう)について

①禅宗では、言葉では言いつくせない真理を坐禅による修行で得ようとします。②だからといって、経典をおろそかにすることはありません。③寺では朝夕の勤行(ごんぎょう)と食事の前のお勤(つと)めとして読経をします。

④よく読まれる経は、「四弘誓願文(しぐせいがんもん)」と「般若心経(はんにゃしんぎょう)」です。

⑤四弘誓願とは、修行者が仏道を求めるときに立てる、追求するべき四つの誓願のことです。「衆生無辺誓願度(しゅじょうむへんせいがんど)(地上にいるあらゆる生き物をすべて救済するという誓願)、煩悩無尽誓願断(ぼんのうむじんせいがんだん)(煩悩は無量だが、すべて断つという誓願)、法門無量誓願学(ほうもんむりょうせいがんがく)(法門は無尽だが、すべて知るという誓願)、仏道無上誓願成(ぶつどうむじょうせいがんじょう)(仏の道は無上だが、必ず成仏するという誓願)」という四つの誓願です。

⑥般若心経は、日本人にもっとも親しまれている経です。⑦日本で唱えられているのは、唐の玄奘(げんじょう)法師がサンスクリット語から、中国語に訳したものです。⑧262文字の短い文の中に、釈迦の教えがすべて入っています。

Heart Sutra / 般若心経

① Avalokiteshvara (アヴァロキテーシュヴァラ), the Bodhisattva (ボディサットヴァ) of Compassion, deep into
観自在菩薩　　　　　　　　　　　　　　菩薩　　　　　　　　慈悲　　　　深く遠くに行く
the Perfection Transcendent of Wisdom, saw clearly that the five
卓越した智慧の完成(→般若波羅蜜多)
aggregates of human existence were empty, and so released himself
五つの集合体(→五蘊)　人間の存在　　　　空　　　　　解き放たれる
from suffering. ② Sariputra! Form is nothing more than emptiness,
　　　苦しみ　　　　　舎利子よ　　形あるもの(→色) ～でしかない　　実体がない(→空)
emptiness is nothing more than Form. ③ Form is exactly emptiness,
　　　　　　　　　　　　　　　　　　　　　　　　　　　　すなわち
and emptiness is exactly Form.　④ The other four aggregates of
human existence — feeling, thought, will, and consciousness are
　　　　　　　　　　感受作用　知覚作用　意志作用　　認識作用
also emptiness. ⑤ Sariputra! All things are empty: ⑥ Nothing is born,
　　　　　　　　　　　　　　　　　　　　　　　　　　　　　何も～でない
nothing dies, nothing is stained, nothing is pure, nothing increases
　　　　　　　　　　　　　　汚れた　　　　　　　　　　　　　　　　増える
and nothing decreases.
　　　　　　減る
⑦ So, in emptiness, there is no form, no feeling, no thought, no
will, no consciousness.　⑧ There are no eyes, no ears, no nose,
no tongue, no body, no mind.　⑨ There is no seeing, no hearing,
　　　　　　　　　　　　　　　　　　　　　　　　　視覚　　　　聴覚
no smelling, no tasting, no touching, no imagining. ⑩ No plane of
　嗅覚　　　　味覚　　　　触覚　　　　意識で感じること　　　次元(→世界)
sight, no plane of thought. ⑪ There is no ignorance, and no end to
目に見えること　　　思考　　　　　　　　　　　無知　　　　　　　　～の終わりがない
ignorance. ⑫ There is no old age and death, and no end to old age

---

①観自在菩薩。行深般若波羅蜜多時。照見五蘊皆空。度一切苦厄。
②舎利子。色不異空。空不異色。③色即是空。空即是色。④受想
行識。亦復如是。⑤舎利子。是諸法空相。⑥不生不滅。不垢不浄。
不増不減。⑦是故空中無色。無受想行識。⑧無眼耳鼻舌身意。
⑨無色声香味触法。⑩無眼界。乃至無意識界。⑪無無明。亦無無
明尽。⑫乃至無老死。亦無老死尽。

78

and death. ⑬There is no suffering, no cause of suffering, no end to suffering, no path to suffering. ⑭There is no attainment of wisdom, and no wisdom to attain." ⑮The Bodhisattvas rely on the Perfection Transcendent of Wisdom, their hearts without delusions; they have no reason for delusion, no fear within, abandoning their confused thoughts, finally experiencing Nirvana. ⑯The Buddhas, past, present, and future, rely on the Perfection Transcendent of Wisdom, and live in full enlightenment. ⑰The Perfection Transcendent of Wisdom is the greatest mantra. ⑱It is the wisest mantra, the highest mantra, the mantra of the rest. It removes all suffering. ⑲This is truth that cannot be doubted. ⑳This is the reason for the Perfection Transcendent of Wisdom Mantra.

The Mantra is thus: Gaté, gaté, paragaté, parasamgaté. Bodhi! Svaha!

(Wikisorce: The Heart Sutra)

---

⑬無苦集滅道。⑭無智亦無得。以無所得故。⑮菩提薩埵。依般若波羅蜜多故。心無罣礙。無罣礙故。無有恐怖。遠離一切顛倒夢想。究竟涅槃。⑯三世諸仏。依般若波羅蜜多故。得阿耨多羅三藐三菩提。⑰故知般若波羅蜜多。是大神呪。⑱是大明呪。是無上呪。是無等等呪。能除一切苦。⑲真実不虚。⑳故説般若波羅蜜多呪。即説呪曰。羯諦。羯諦。波羅羯諦。波羅僧羯諦。菩提薩婆訶。般若心経。

（ウィキソース「般若心経」を参考にして作成）

People Influenced by Zen / 禅の影響を受けた人々②

Ii Naosuke / 井伊 直弼(いい なおすけ)

It was *Ii Naoske*, the *tairo* or the Chief minister of the Shogunate, who decided to open the country at the end of the *Edo* period. *Naosuke*, born as the fourteenth son of *Hikone-han*'s domain lord, had no possibility to become an heir. At the age of thirteen, he started to train in the *Seiryo-ji* Zen temple, the *Ii* family temple. After the death of his father, at seventeen years old, he began living in a house outside the castle according to the laws of the local government. Although he was suffering economically, he was absorbed in studying and training in the martial arts; and strict zazen training as well. As a result, he received certification from Master *Senei*. It was "Zen's mind" that sustained him until his death. Before completing the Treaty of Amity and Commerce between the United States of America and the Empire of Japan, he had been uncertain about the decision. The master's words, "Only one word, 'decide' will be left, if you strip away unnecessary thoughts" helped *Naoske* make the decision.

江戸末期に開国を決めたのは、大老・井伊直弼でした。彦根藩主の14番目の子として生まれた直弼には、跡取りになる可能性がありませんでした。直弼は13歳から、井伊家の菩提寺の禅寺である清涼寺で修行しました。父の死後、17歳で藩の掟により城外で一人暮らしを始めます。経済的には苦しかったにもかかわらず、文武を修めることに専心するとともに、坐禅の厳しい修行を続けました。その結果、仙英禅師より印可を受けました。

最後まで直弼の精神的な支えになったのが、禅の心です。日米修好通商条約を締結する際、心が揺れていました。禅師の「心頭を滅却し、ただ断の一字あるのみ」という言葉により、直弼は心を決めました。

出典:『いわみガイド』鳥取県岩美町制作

Chapter 4

Interpretation
of Ten Bulls

....

第4章
『十牛図』を読み解く

Zen Buddhism

30 What Is "Ten Bulls"?

① In the twelfth century, *Kakuan* (廊庵), a Chinese Zen master, drew ten drawings (絵画) of bulls with texts (文章) as teaching material (教材) for Zen students.

② This is "Ten Bulls".

③ Each of the ten drawings has two short texts, "*jo*" (序), "an introduction" (導入) and "*jyu*" (頌), "a poem" (詩); a *jo* is a brief summary (簡単な要約) of the drawing and a *jyu* is a poem describing (表現している) the scene of the drawing.

④ In China during the *Sòng* Dynasty (中国の宋の時代に), this style was common (一般的な) to describe (表す) the "mind of Buddha" and a stage (段階) of enlightenment (悟り).

⑤ "Ten Bulls" illustrated (図解した) the process where a cowboy (牧童) lost his bull, searched for it (〜を探す) and caught it. ⑥ The bull is actually (実際には) a symbol (象徴) of "the nature of the self" which can be said is "a

82

mind of emptiness" in Buddhism.
　　　　　　　　　空っぽであること
⑦The ten illustrations lead the trainees step by step to
　　　　　　　　　　　導く　修行する人　　段階的に
enlightenment.

⑧I will explain each "*jo*" and "*jyu*" separately for each of
　　　　　　　　　　　　　　　　　別々に
the ten illustrations in the following pages.
　　　　　　　　　　次のページから

30.『十牛図』とは何か？

①12世紀の中国の禅僧廓庵は、禅を学ぶ人のために10枚の絵と漢文からなる絵物語をつくりました。

②これが『十牛図』です。

③10枚の絵にそれぞれ、その絵の意図を簡潔に述べてある「序」と、内容を物語風の漢詩で表現している「頌」という短文がついています。

④中国では宋の時代に、このような漢詩の形態で仏心を示したり、悟りの境地を表すことが広く行なわれていました。

⑤十牛図は、牛を見失った牛飼いの牧童が、牛を探し捕えるまでの過程を描いています。⑥牛は、実際には人間が持つ「本来の自分」、つまり仏教における「空の心」を象徴しています。

⑦牧童が牛を探す道程を表した10枚の絵は、禅の悟りへと段階的に導くためのものです。

⑧次のページから10枚の絵についてそれぞれ、「序」と「頌」に分けて解説していきます。

31　No.1 "Searching for the Bull"

①The cowboy is searching for the
　牧童　　　　　　　　探す
bull. ②The bull represents the true
　　牛　　　　　表わしている　　真実の
mind of the cowboy.

【Introduction】

③The bull has never been lost. ④What need is there for me to
　　　　　　　　　　　　　　　　　何のために
search? ⑤When I was looking the other way, the bull left and
　　　　　　　　　　　　　　　反対の方向を
I lost sight of him in the dust. ⑥It is far from home, I see many
　　見失った　　　　ほこりの中で
crossroads, but which way is the right one I do not know.
岐路
⑦Thoughts about gain and loss arise, like dagger points of
　　考え　　　　　　得るもの　失うもの 生じる　　　　短刀の先
good and bad thoughts in my life.
善と悪の考え(→是非の思い)

【Poem】

⑧In this field, I push aside the tall grasses growing thick
　　　　野原　　脇に押しのける　　　　　　　　　　　　密集して
and wild in search of the bull. ⑨Wide rivers are flowing,
　　　自然に　～を探し求めて　　　　　　　　　　　　　流れる

84

there is a path leading to the far distant mountains. ⑩My
　　　　　　　　　　　　道　　　　　　　　はるか遠く
strength is running out and my mind is exhausted, I cannot
力　　　　　使い果たして　　　　　　　　　シケイダス　疲れて
find the bull. ⑪I only hear the cicadas buzzing through the
　　　　　　　　　　　　　　　蝉　　　　　鳴いている
forest of maple trees at night.
森　　　　楓の木

---

31. 第一図「尋牛（じんぎゅう）」

①牧童が牛を探しています。②牛は「本来の自分の心」を表しています。

【序】
③もともと牛はいなくなってはいないのだ。④何のために探す必要があるのか。⑤牛に背を向けたので、牛は離れてしまい、ほこりで視界がとざされてついに見失ってしまった。⑥故郷からどんどん遠ざかってしまい、道の分岐点で途方に暮れる。⑦物事の得失を判断する思いが火のように燃え上がり、是非の思いが刃物の先のように鋭く起こる。

【頌】
⑧野原にうっそうと茂る草を押しのけて、牛を追って進む。⑨広い川が流れ、道ははるか遠く山に向かって続いている。⑩力が尽きてしまい、精神が疲れて牛を見つけることができない。⑪夕方になって、楓（かえで）の木の森に蝉（せみ）が鳴いているのをただ聞いている。

32 No.2 "Discovering the Footprints"

①He finds the footprints of the
           足跡
bull in the field where the grasses

are growing close together.
       生い茂って
②Therefore, he finds a clue to his
  すなわち   手がかり
true mind.
本当の心

【Introduction】

③I devote myself to the sutra and after reading the
   ～に没頭する
Buddhist scriptures, I come to understand the teaching; I
仏教の経典   ～になる   教え
see the footprints of the bull. ④Then I realize that, just as
                                    わかる あたかも～のように
many utensils are made from one metal, so there are
ユーテンシルズ
    器   ～からつくられる 金属
countless existences made of oneself. ⑤Unless I judge
無数の   ～することなしには
between right and wrong, I cannot realize the facts. ⑥I

have not yet entered the gate, however I recognize the tracks.
                                         わかる   道筋

【Poem】

⑦Along a riverfront under the trees, there are many
川岸沿いに

86

第4章 『十牛図』を読み解く

footprints. ⑧The bull has found fragrant grasses growing
　　　　　　　　　　　　　　　　　いい香りのする草
in the field. ⑨Even if the bull is deep in the mountains, it
　　　　　　　　　　　　　　　　　　山奥に
will be found. ⑩The bull's nose looking towards heaven;
nobody can hide him.
誰も隠すことはできない

---

32. 第二図「見跡(けんせき)」

①草の生(お)い茂る野原の中で牛の足跡を見つけます。②すなわち、自分の本当の心の手がかりを見つけたのです。

【序】
③経典を読んで教えを理解し、経典に没頭することで牛の足跡を見つけた。④そして私は、いろいろな器(うつわ)が一つの金属でできているように、すべてのものも自分と同じであることがわかった。⑤正しいことと間違っていることを判断できないのに、私は真実か偽(いつわ)りかを理解できない。⑥まだその門をくぐっていないのだが、牛の足跡を見つけることはできる。

【頌】
⑦水辺の木々の下には、たくさんの足跡があった。⑧牛はその香りがいい草が野原一面に育っているのを見たに違いない。⑨たとえ山奥にいるとしても、牛は見つかるだろう。⑩牛は鼻先を天に向けて進んでいるので、誰も牛を隠すことはできない。

33　No.3 "Perceiving the Bull"
気づくこと

①The cowboy follows the footprints and finally finds the bull.
②He could see the true mind deep inside himself.

【Introduction】

③If one hears the voice, then one can recognize what the source is.
　　　　　　　　　　　　　　　　　　　　～がわかる
出どころ

④What one gets from each of the six senses are the same.
　　　　　　　　　　　　　　　六感

⑤There is some salt in the sea water, and there is some glue in the paint.
　　　　　　　　　　　　　　　　　　　　　　　　　　　　膠
塗料

⑥You can see the object as it is, only when you observe it.
　　　　　　　もの　　あるがままに　　　　　　～をよく観察する

【Poem】

⑦I can hear a black-naped Oriole singing on the tip of a branch.
　　　　　　　コウライウグイス　　　　　　　　　先
枝

88

⑧The sun is warm, the wind is mild, willows are green along the shore.
柳　　　　　　　　岸辺の
⑨No bulls can hide here anymore.
隠れる
⑩But one can only draw with difficulty, those majestic horns.
描く　かろうじて〜できる　　　　堂々とした　角

---

33. 第三図「見牛（けんぎゅう）」

①牧童は牛の足跡をたどり、ついに牛の姿を見つけます。②自分の中にある本当の心を見ることができたのです。

【序】
③声を聞けば、その出どころがわかる。
④六感のそれぞれから得たものは、異なる（こと）ものではない。
⑤海水の中には塩分があり、絵の具には膠（にかわ）が入っている。
⑥よく見ることによって、ものの真の姿が見える。

【頌】
⑦黄色の鶯（うぐいす）が枝先でさえずっている。
⑧陽（ひ）は暖かく風は穏やかで、岸辺の柳も青々としている。
⑨もうどんな牛も隠れることはできない。
⑩それでも堂々とつき出た角（つの）を、描ける人はなかなかいない。

34 No.4 "Catching the Bull"

①Though the cowboy is trying to catch the bull, it violently resists him. ②It is difficult to keep firm control of one's true mind completely.
- violently 激しく
- resists ~に抵抗する
- keep firm control ~をしっかりと支配する
- completely 完全に

【Introduction】

③The bull had hidden in the country for a long time: I finally saw him today.
- finally ついに

④Confused by my surroundings, it's difficult for me to catch the bull.
- Confused 混乱して
- surroundings 周囲の環境

⑤The bull always longs for fragrant grasses, and he stays there.
- longs for 恋しがる
- fragrant grasses いい香りの草

⑥His mind still is stubborn and his nature is still wild.
- stubborn 頑固で

⑦I must raise my whip, if I wish him to submit.
- raise ~を高くあげる
- whip 鞭
- submit 服従させる

【Poem】

⑧I catch the bull after a tremendous struggle.
- tremendous ものすごい
- struggle 奮闘

⑨The bull's great will and power can hardly be taken from him.

⑩Sometimes the bull suddenly climbs to a high plateau, or he goes into the deep fog and stays quietly.
　　　　　　　　　突然　　　　　　　　高原

34. 第四図「得牛」

①牛を捕まえようとしますが、牛は激しく抵抗します。②自分の本当の心を完全に掌握するのは難しいのです。

【序】
③牛は長い間、野外の草むらに隠れていたが、今日出会えた。
④私はまわりの環境によって混乱して、牛を捕まえるのが難しい。
⑤牛はいい香りの草を恋しがり、そこにいる。
⑥牛の心はまだ頑固で野生のままだ。
⑦飼いならそうとすれば、私は鞭で打たなければならない。
【頌】
⑧私は牛を必死にもがいて捕まえる。
⑨牛の強い意志と力を取り除くことはできない。
⑩牛は突然高原に登ったかと思えば、霧の奥深いところに入ってじっとしていたりする。

35   No.5 "Taming the Bull"

①Though you can tame the raging bull, you have to be very alert. ②It is important for you to maintain your inner serenity.

【Introduction】

③When one thought arises, another thought follows.
④A truth is what you realize as a truth.
⑤It would be illusion, if you had a doubt about it.
⑥A truth exists not because of the surroundings but because of oneself.

⑦Hold tight to the bull by the nose-ring and do not allow even a doubt.

【Poem】

⑧The whip and rope are necessary for the cowboy.

第4章 『十牛図』を読み解く

⑨Or else the bull might stray off down some dusty road.
　　さもなければ　　　　　　　　離れる　　　　　　　　ほこりっぽい
⑩Being well trained, the bull becomes naturally gentle.
　　　　　　　　　　　　　　　　　　　　　　　　穏やかな
⑪Then, unfettered, he obeys his master.
　　　　　拘束されなくても　従う

35. 第五図「牧牛(ぼくぎゅう)」

①あばれ牛を飼いならすことができましたが、油断は禁物です。
②自分の心を安定させることが大事なのです。

【序】
③一つの考えが起こったら、次から次へと考えが続いて起きてしまうものだ。
④自分が真実だと理解したものが真実なのだ。
⑤事実について疑いの気持ちを持てば、幻(まぼろし)になるだろう。
⑥真実は、周囲によって存在するのではなく、自分自身によって存在する。
⑦牛の鼻輪をしっかり握って、少しの疑問も許さないことだ。

【頌】
⑧牧童には鞭(むち)と手綱(たづな)が必要だ。
⑨さもなければ、牛は離れて、ほこりっぽい道に入るに違いない。
⑩しかし、よく手なずけると、牛は自然に穏やかになる。
⑪こうなれば、自由にしておいても牛は主(あるじ)に従うようになる。

93

36 No.6 "Riding the Bull Home"

①On the bull's back, the cowboy goes home at a slow pace. ②The bull does not show violent behavior nor run away any more.

【Introduction】

③Now the struggle is over; no need to think about gain and loss any more.
④I sing the song of the village woodsman and whistle the tunes of the children.
⑤Riding the bull, I see the clouds above.
⑥I go forward, no matter who calls me back, no matter what attracts me.

【Poem】

⑦Riding the bull, I return homeward, peacefully.

第4章 『十牛図』を読み解く

⑧The voice of my flute sounds in the evening mist.
　音　　　　　　　　　　鳴り響く　　　　　　霞
⑨Each beat of my rhythm and the song I'm singing has eternal meaning.
永遠の
⑩No explanation is needed for the people who know this sound.
どんな説明も〜ない

36. 第六図「騎牛帰家（きぎゅうきけ）」

①牛の背に乗ってゆっくりと家に帰ります。②牛はもうあばれたり逃げたりしません。

【序】
③牛との格闘はもう終わり、もう得ることと失うことで考える必要はなくなった。
④村の木こりの唱歌を歌い、子どもが野原で奏（かな）でる曲を笛で吹く。
⑤牛の背に乗って、頭上の雲をながめる。
⑥誰かが戻っておいでと言っても戻らないし、何が引き止めても、とどまらない。

【頌】
⑦牛に乗って穏やかな気持ちで家に帰る。
⑧私が吹く横笛の音が夕方の霞（かすみ）の中で響く。
⑨私が奏でる拍子と歌の一つひとつに、限りない意味がある。
⑩この音色（ねいろ）を知（い）っている人には説明など要らないのだ。

37 No.7 "The Bull Transcended"
超越した(→なくなった)

①The bull went somewhere, though the boy had caught it.
　　　　　　　どこかに
　～だが
②And the boy feels at ease as if he forgets to achieve enlightenment.
　　　　　のんびりとする

【Introduction】

③As all is one law, not two, the bull is a symbol of them.
　～なので　　　法　　　　　　　　　　　　　　象徴
④The bull is like a trap to catch rabbits and like a bamboo basket to catch fish.
　　　　　～のようだ　罠　　　　　　ウサギ　　　　竹で編んだかご
　　　　　　　　　魚
⑤It is like gold emerging from mineral, and like the moon emerging from a cloud.
　　　　　　　　～から出てくる　鉱物

⑥The dim moonlight has been seen since a long time ago.
　　　ほの暗い　　　　　　見られている

【Poem】

⑦Riding the bull, I have reached home.

⑧The bull is empty and my mind is peaceful.
　　　　　　空っぽになる(→姿を消す)　　穏やかだ

⑨Though the sun is already high in the sky, I feel like I am dreaming.

⑩I have abandoned the whip and rope in my thatched hut.
　　　捨ててしまった　　　　　　　　　　　　　　　　わらぶき小屋

37. 第七図「忘牛存人(ぼうぎゅうそんにん)」

①捕まえた牛はどこかに行ってしまいました。
②牧童は悟ったことも忘れるくらい、のんびりしています。

【序】
③法は二つはなく、一つしかないもので、牛はその真理の象徴である。④牛は、ウサギを捕まえる罠(わな)や、魚を獲(と)る竹かごのようなものである。
⑤それは、鉱物の中からとり出される金(きん)のようなものであり、雲の合間から現れる月のようなものだ。⑥ほの暗い月明かりは太古(たいこ)の昔から見られていたものだ。

【頌】
⑦牛に乗って家に帰ってきた。
⑧牛は姿を消したが、私の心は穏やかだ。
⑨太陽がもうすでに空高くのぼっているけれども、私は夢の中にいるようだ。
⑩私はわらぶき小屋に、鞭(むち)と手綱(たづな)をほうり投げた。

97

38　No.8 "Both Bull and Self Transcended"

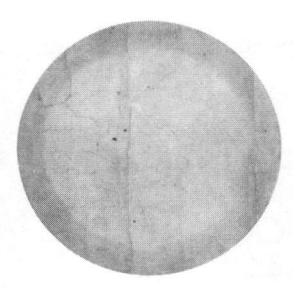

①Both the bull and the cowboy have disappeared.
消える
②They enter into the zone of emptiness where one forgets one's enlightened existence.
からっぽの　　　　　　～を忘れる
悟った存在

【Introduction】

③Not only is my mind of mediocrity gone, I don't have a
～だけでなく　　　　　平凡
holy mind anymore. ④I am not playing at the place where
神聖な
enlightenment is, I pass quickly through the place of no
悟り
enlightenment. ⑤Since I do not stay in either condition, no eyes can catch me. ⑥If birds knew I attained enlightenment, they would bring me flowers. ⑦Such praise would be
賞賛
meaningless though.
意味のない

【Poem】

⑧The whip, the rope, the person, and the bull, all are gone
鞭

now. ⑨The clear, blue sky spreads out so far that I can send a message to no one. ⑩How can a snowflake exist in a raging fire? ⑪Here, I reach the point where the master has led me.

あまりにも－なので / 雪片 / 存在する / 燃えさかる

---

38. 第八図「人牛倶忘(じんぎゅうぐぼう)」

①牛も牧童もいなくなりました。②悟(さと)った自分の存在も忘れてしまう「空(くう)」の状態です。

【序】
③凡庸(ぼんよう)な気持ちだけではなく、仏の心までもなくなってしまった。④悟りのあるところで遊ぶこともなく、悟りのないところはさっと通り抜ける。⑤どちらの場所にもいないから、どんな目で見張っていても私を捕まえることはできない。⑥鳥たちは私が悟りの境地に達したのを知ったら、花を持ってきてくれるだろう。⑦そんな賞賛は意味のないことではあるけれど。

【頌】
⑧鞭(むち)も手綱(たづな)も人も牛も、いまやすべてなくなってしまった。⑨透(す)き通った空がはるか遠くまで広がっていて、誰にもメッセージを伝えられない。⑩燃えさかる炎の中で、どうやって雪を解(と)かさないでおくことができるのだろうか。⑪ここにきて私は、祖師(そし)が導いた境地に着いたのだ。

39 No.9 "Reaching the Source"
源にたどり着く(→還源)

① Rivers flow as they are and flowers bloom without intention.
あるがままに　　　　　　　花を咲かせる　　　　　意思

② The cowboy becomes aware that the truth is the world which he is just seeing.
　　　　　　～であることに気がつく

【Introduction】

③ The self is naturally clean and innocent.

④ Objects, which have forms, rise and fall; finally reaching the stage of nothingness.
形　　　上がり下がりがある(→栄枯盛衰がある)
何もないこと(→無)

⑤ Since this stage is not illusion, I do not have to train myself any more.
幻

⑥ The water of the rivers is ever green and the mountains are ever blue; the only thing to do now is to observe them.
観察する

【Poem】

⑦ Having returned to the origin, how much I elaborated
根源的なところ　　　　　　念入りに工夫した

100

variously and spent time in vain.
　　さまざまに　　　　　　　　　　むだに
⑧ It would have been better that I was blind and deaf.
　　　　　　　　　　　　　　　　　　　目が見えない　耳が聞こえない
⑨ Being in the hut, I could see nothing.
　　　　　　　小屋(庵)
⑩ Such as water flowing and the red flowers in bloom.
たとえば〜など

39. 第九図「返本還源(へんぽんかんげん)」

①川はあるがままに流れ、花は無心に咲きます。②牧童は見たままの世界が真実なのだと気づくのです。

【序】
③本来の自己は、清らかで塵(ちり)一つない。④形ある物の栄枯盛衰を見て、無の境地に落ち着く。⑤これは幻ではないのだから、もう私は精進(しょうじん)する必要はない。⑥川の水は緑で山は青い、居ながらにして万物の成り行きを観察するだけだ。

【頌】
⑦もとに戻り、もっと根源的なところに還(かえ)ってくると、これまで自分はなんと工夫をこらし、いろいろと費(つい)やしてきたことか。⑧最初から目が見えなくて耳が聞こえない人であったほうがよかった。⑨庵(いおり)の中にいて、外にあるものは何も見えなかった。
⑩今は、水は自然にさらさら流れ、花はもともと赤い色をしているのが見える。

No.10 "In the World"
世の中で(→普通の暮らしに戻る)

①Not showing his enlightened face, he returned to the ordinary life. ②So that he can offer a helping hand to those who need his help.

【Introduction】

③Closing my brushwood gate, I do not tell even the wise men where I am. ④Hiding the light emanating from my body, I refuse to follow the way of the wise men. ⑤I go to town carrying a gourd for a canteen and I come back home with the help of a stick.

⑥If I see the people in a liquor shop or fish market, I influence them and lead them to enlightenment.

【Poem】

⑦Exposing my chest and with bare feet, I go into the market.

第4章 『十牛図』を読み解く

⑧I am covered with mud and ash, but I have a full smile on my face.
　　　～で覆われている　　泥　　　灰

⑨I don't need the help of the secret power of hermits.
　　　　　　　　　　　　　　　　　　　　　　　　　　仙人

⑩I can make the flowers bloom on a dead tree.
　　　～を―させる　　　　　咲く　　　枯れ木

40. 第十図「入鄽垂手(にってんすいしゅ)」

①悟りを得た顔をしないようにして、普通の暮らしに戻ります。②そうすることで、助けを求める人に手をさし伸べることができるのです。

【序】
③柴(しば)の戸を一人閉ざして、どんな賢人にも知らさない。
④自分の輝きを隠し、賢人の歩んだ道をも拒(こば)む。
⑤ひょうたんをぶら下げて街に行き、杖(つえ)をついて家に帰る。
⑥酒屋、魚屋で出会った人を感化して、悟りに導く。
【頌】
⑦胸をあらわにして、裸足(はだし)で店に入ってくる。
⑧土にまみれ、灰をかぶりながらも顔じゅうを口のようにして笑っている。
⑨神秘的な仙人の秘密の力などは使わない。
⑩すぐに枯れ木に花を咲かせてみせる。

103

People Influenced by Zen / 禅の影響を受けた人々③

San-yutei Encho 三遊亭 圓朝

San-yutei Enchō is a *rakugoka* (a comic story teller), who actively performed from the end of the shogunate age to the *Meiji* period; He is also known as the author of the ghost stories "*Kaidan Botan Dōrō*" and "*Shinkei Kasanegafuchi*". Born as a son of a *rakugoka*, he started his career at the age of six, then he entered a temple to nurture his versatility when he was fourteen years old. As an adolescent, his talent flourished and he climbed to the top, however he returned to Zen training at the age of thirty-seven. It was *Yamaoka Tesshū*'s words that led him to return to Zen training. *Tesshū* criticized *Enchō*'s performance harshly saying that "The story you tell is dead because you are telling it only with your tongue"; he recommended that *Enchō* train in a Zen temple. The two of them trained in a temple of the *Rinzai* school together. *Enchō*, there, learned the "mind of Zen"; which intensified his unique style of "getting into character".

三遊亭圓朝は、幕末から明治にかけて活躍した落語家で、「怪談牡丹燈籠」や「真景累ヶ淵」の原作者としても知られています。落語家の子として生まれ、6歳で落語家になった圓朝は、落語がうまくなるようにと14歳から禅寺に入りました。青年期には才覚を発揮して、落語界の頂点にまで上りつめますが、37歳のときに再び禅の修行を始めます。そのきっかけとなったのは、山岡鉄舟との出会いでした。鉄舟は、圓朝を「舌の先だけでしゃべっていて人物が死んでいる」と酷評し、禅寺で修行することを勧めました。圓朝は鉄舟とともに臨済宗の寺で禅を修行しました。そこで禅の心を会得した圓朝は、徹底して話中の「人物になりきる」独自の芸風を深めました。

Chapter **5**

Reading Kōan

....

第5章
「公案」を読む

Zen Buddhism

41   What is Kōan?

①*Kōans* are questions which are posed by a Zen master for the trainee to attain enlightenment. ②*Kōans* always contain contradictions to common knowledge. ③The trainee is forced to concentrate on the *kōan* so that he extinguishes his "self".

④The correct answer is decided by the master; a universal answer does not exist. ⑤The trainee states his well thought out answer to the master but the answer is refused and thrown back almost every time. ⑥In some cases, the trainee continues to consider a *kōan* for some years. ⑦The more answers the trainee gives, the closer he approaches to enlightenment. ⑧The master instructs the trainee to reach the ultimate stage of Zen through *kōans*.

⑨*Kōans* originate from sources such as Buddhist sutras and quotations from eminent priests from the *Song* Dynasty in China. ⑩"*Mumonkan*" was compiled by *Mumon Ekai*, a

Zen priest of the *Song* Dynasty. ⑪"*Hekiganroku*" was compiled by *Engo Kokugon*, also a Zen priest of the *Song* Dynasty. ⑫"*Rinzairoku*" is a book containing the quotations from *Rinzai Gigen* who is the founder of the *Rinzai* school.

41. 公案とは

①公案とは、禅の修行者が悟りを開くために、師によって与えられる問題のことです。②公案は常に一般常識とは矛盾した内容を含んでいます。③修行者は公案に集中せざるを得ず、自己を消し去ることを強いられます。

④正解は師が決めることで、模範解答はありません。⑤修行者は、いく度となく工夫した答えを師にぶつけては否定され跳ね返されることを繰り返します。⑥ときには修行者は、一つの公案を何年間も考え抜くこともあります。⑦いくつもの公案を解答することで悟りに近づいていきます。⑧師は、公案を通じて修行者を悟りの境地へと導きます。

⑨公案は、仏教の経典や、中国の宋の時代につくられた高僧の語録などが出典となっています。⑩『無門関』は、中国の宋時代の禅僧、無門慧開によって編集されました。⑪同じく宋の禅僧である圜悟克勤によって『碧巌録』がつくられました。⑫『臨済録』は臨済宗の開祖である臨済義玄の語録です。

42 　　　　　　*Joshū's* Dog

①One day a priest asked Master *Joshū*: "Does a dog have the "mind of Buddha" or not?"
②*Joshū* answered: "*mu* (nothingness)".
③This is the most well known *kōan*, which is given to a trainee who practices zazen for the first time. ④Although *Gautama Siddhārtha* taught that all the creatures had the "mind of Buddha", why did he answer "*mu*"?
⑤"*Mu*" does not mean the same as "not exist" of "exist or not exist". ⑥It is wasteful to try to understand this "*mu*". ⑦All you have to do is to concentrate on "nothingness" until you become aware of something. ⑧It is so difficult to understand "*mu*" therefore many trainees suffer from it.
⑨*Mumon Ekai*, the editor of "*Mumonkan*", advised as follows:
⑩"When you challenge this *kōan*, you must not focus on "exist or not exist". ⑪Harmful knowledge will be washed

out cleanly when you pass this barrier; you should feel like drinking a hot iron ball that you can neither swallow nor spit out. ⑫Recite repeatedly, "*mu, mu, mu*" until this moment."

---

42. 狗子仏性（『無門関』一則）

①ある日、一人の僧が趙州和尚に尋ねた。「犬には仏性が有るでしょうか、それとも無いでしょうか」
②趙州は「無」と答えた。
③これは、一番有名な公案で、禅の修行をする人が最初に与えられるものです。④釈迦はすべての生物に仏性があると説いたのに、なぜ「無」なのでしょうか。
⑤「無」は、有るとか無いとかの「無」ではないのです。⑥頭で理解しようとしても無駄です。⑦何かの気づきがあるまで、「無」に心を集中させるしかありません。⑧この「無」を理解するのは、簡単なことではないので、たくさんの修行者が苦しみます。⑨『無門関』の編者である無門慧開が、こう助言しています。⑩「この公案を修行するにあたっては、有るとか無いとかにこだわってはいけない。⑪真っ赤に焼けた鉄の固まりを飲み込んだように、吐き出そうにも吐き出すことができない状態をすぎると、悪い知識がすっかり洗い尽くされる。⑫それまで、ずっと無、無、無と唱え続けなさい」

43 *Joshū* Washes a Bowl

①A priest came to see *Joshū* and said to him: "I have just entered the monastery. ②Please show me the way I should go."

③*Joshū* asked: "Have you eaten your rice porridge?"

④The priest replied: "I have eaten."

⑤*Joshū* said: "Then you had better wash your bowl."

At that moment the priest was enlightened.

⑥What did *Joshū* intend to say in this *kōan*?

⑦The followings are three examples of different interpretations.

⑧As the fundament of Zen training is to concentrate on the daily work, the significance is just in the trivial work.

⑨You should find the way yourself; it is not a subject for which to pose a question to anyone else.

⑩To compare a bowl to the head, it is important to keep it clean and empty.

110

⑪However, these may not be correct answers when you
　　　　　しかしながら　　　　　　～とは限らない
study this *kōan*, in practicing Zen.

43. 趙州洗鉢(じょうしゅうせんぱつ)（『無門関』七則）

①趙州のもとに一人の僧が来て、「私は道場に来たばかりの新参者です。②進むべき道を教えてください」と言いました。③趙州は、「朝の粥(かゆ)は食べたか」と尋ねました。④僧は、「食べました」と答えました。⑤「それなら、お椀(わん)を洗っておきなさい」と趙州が言ったとき、その僧は悟りました。

⑥この公案で、趙州が言いたかったことは、どんなことなのでしょうか。

⑦次に、三つの解釈をあげます。

⑧日常の仕事に専心するのが修行の基本であり、些細(ささい)な仕事の中にこそ意義があるのだということ、⑨進むべき道は、自分でなんとか考えるもので、教えを請(こ)うものではないということ、⑩お椀を自分の頭になぞらえて、空っぽにしてきれいにしておくことが大事だということ。

⑪ただし、これらが必ずしも公案の修行をするときの正解というわけではありません。

111

44 *Hyakujō's* Wild Fox

①Here, I introduce a summary of the beginning of this *kōan* because it is very long. ②There had been an old man who was always present at *Hyakujō's* preaching. ③When *Hyakujō* asked his background, he began his story: ④"A long time ago, I had been a priest of this temple, but now, I'm not a human being. ⑤One day, an old man asked me whether a man who was enlightened does not adhere to the rule of cause and effect or does he rise above it. ⑥I answered by mistake that he does not adhere to the rule of causality. ⑦As a result, I was born again and again as a wild fox five hundred times. ⑧Please say the correct word for me and rescue me." ⑨When *Hyakujō* told him that no one can escape from the rule of causality, the old man was enlightened and became a human being. ⑩If you are enlightened,

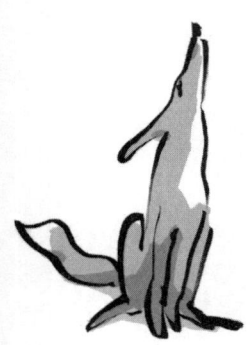

you do not have to adhere to either the law of causality or
                                   ──────────────────────
                                        因果律
the differentiation. ⑪It is the "way of Buddha" to live as
───────────────────
       分別
well as possible in your role, even if you become a wild fox.
できる限り最善に   役割(立場)

44. 百丈野狐(ひゃくじょうやこ)(『無門関』二則)

①この公案はとても長いので、前半の部分のあらすじだけを紹介します。

②百丈の説法にいつも現れる老人がいました。③百丈が老人の身の上を尋ねると、老人は次のように話し始めました。

「④私は昔、この寺の住職でしたが、いまは人間ではありません。⑤ある僧が、悟りの極致に至った人は因果の法則に囚われないか、それとも因果の法則を超越しているのかと私に尋ねました。⑥私は、因果の法則には囚われません(不落因果(ふらくいんが))と誤(あやま)って答えてしまいました。⑦そのため、私は500回も野狐に生まれ変わっています。⑧私の代わりに正しい言葉を説き、この身を救ってください」

⑨百丈が、因果の法則から逃れることはできない(不昧因果(ふまいいんが))と答えると、老人は悟りを開き、野狐から人間に戻りました。⑩悟りを開けば、因果律にも分別(ふんべつ)にも囚われることはありません。⑪たとえ野狐に生まれ変わっても、おかれている立場で精一杯生きていれば、それが仏道だということです。

45   *Nansen* Cuts the Cat in Two

①Master *Nansen* saw that the priests of the eastern and western halls had a quarrel over a cat. ②He seized the cat and told the priests: "If any of you say a good word, you can save the cat. If not, I will cut it." ③No one answered, so *Nansen* cut the cat into two pieces.

④That evening *Joshū* returned and *Nansen* told him about this. ⑤*Joshū* removed his sandal, put it on his head, and walked out.

⑥*Nansen* said: "If he had been there, he could have saved the cat."

⑦It is thought that the cat is a symbol of *kleśa*. ⑧The priests having a quarrel could not abandon it. ⑨Master *Nansen* cut the desire in two pieces. ⑩On

第5章 「公案」を読む

the other hand, the odd action of *Joshū* is a warning that we
　その一方で　　　　　　　　　奇妙な　　　　　　　　　　警告
must not hold fast to any idea.
　　　　　執着する

45. 南泉斬猫（『無門関』十四則）

①ある日、東西の僧堂の僧たちが、一匹の猫をめぐって言い争いをしていました。②そのとき南泉和尚は猫をつまみ上げてこう言いました。「おまえたち、禅の道の言葉を何か言うことができるなら、この猫を助けるが、言えなければ、斬り捨てるぞ」
③誰も答えられなかったので、南泉和尚は猫を斬ってしまいました。
④夕方、趙州が外出先から帰ってきたので、南泉は趙州にこの一件を話しました。⑤趙州は履を脱いで、それを自分の頭の上に載せて出て行きました。⑥南泉は、「もし趙州があのときいたなら、猫を救えたのに」と言いました。
⑦猫はここでは、煩悩を表していると考えられます。⑧言い争いをしている僧たちは、それを捨てることができなかったのです。
⑨南泉和尚は煩悩を断ち切りました。⑩一方、趙州の奇妙な行動は、何事にも囚われていてはいけないという戒めです。

46 The Juniper Tree In Front of the Hall

①A priest asked *Joshū* (趙州), "What was the true purpose (目的) for *Bodhidharma* (ボディダーマ/達磨) to come to China from India?" ②*Joshū* answered, "It's a juniper tree (ジャニパー/ビャクシン(柏槇)の木) in front of the garden."

③This *kōan* is asking what is the essence *Bodhidharma* brought from India to China. ④This is the ultimate (究極の) issue (問題) for priests who practice Zen. ⑤It does not simply mean (意味する) that the juniper tree has the "mind of Buddha". ⑥*Mumon* (無門), as the editor (編者), commented (~と解説した), "The words can not transmit (伝える) the real nature of the truth. ⑦You will miss (~を見失う) the truth if you accept the word as it is (ありのままに)".

⑧*Joshū* says that the juniper tree is the ultimate stage (境地) of Zen. ⑨To strive (~するように努力する) decisively (徹底的に) to be a subject (対象) until your body changes into a juniper tree.

⑩Throwing all delusion (妄想) and

116

第5章 「公案」を読む

differentiation and assimilating yourself into the object
区別すること(→分別)　同化する　　　　　　　　　　　　対象
without thinking, you will resonate with the ultimate stage
　　　　　　　　　　　　～と共鳴する
of Zen which *Bodhidharma* experienced.
　　　　　　　　　　経験した

46. 庭前柏樹（ていぜんのはくじゅ）（『無門関』三十七則）

①ある僧が、「達磨大師がインドから中国へ来られた真意は何か」と趙州に尋ねました。②趙州は「庭先にある柏の樹である」と答えました。

③この公案は、祖師達磨がインドから中国に伝えた禅の真髄は何かという問いです。④禅に取り組む人にとって究極の問題です。⑤これは単純にすべての物に仏心があるということではなさそうです。⑥編者の無門がこの公案に関し、「言葉は事実の本質を伝えられない。⑦言葉をそのまま受け取ると真実を見失う」ということを述べています。

⑧趙州は、柏の樹が禅の境地であると述べています。⑨自分の身が柏の樹になるまで、徹底的に対象になろうとすること。⑩妄想と分別のすべてを取り払い、何も考えずに物と自我を一体化させることで、達磨の禅の境地と共鳴できるということです。

47 Progress from the Top of the Pole
歩を進める

①Master *Sekisō* asked; "How do you step forward from the
石霜　　　　　　　　　　　　　　　～に向かってのぼる
top of a hundred foot pole?"
　　　　百尺　　　　　竿

②Another Zen Master of ancient age said; "One who keeps

sitting at top of a hundred foot pole has not attained true
　　　　　　　　　　　　　　　　　　　　　　　～を達成する
enlightenment. ③Make another step forward from the top

of the pole and actualize all your capacity in the whole
　　　　　　　　　実現する　　　　　　能力　　　世界中で
world in all directions."
すべての方向で

④"The top of the hundred foot high pole" is a symbol of
　　　　　　　　　　　　　　　　　　　　　　　　象徴
the stage a trainee has reached.
　　　　　修行者

⑤Even though the trainee has reached this stage, he begins
たとえ～であっても
to hold fast to things when he becomes careless.
　物事にこだわる　　　　　　　注意しなくなる(→気を抜く)

⑥The time after having attained enlightenment is more

important. ⑦He should fly up from the top of the pole.
　　　　　　　　　　　　～から飛ぶ

⑧Then, he should go among the people to save them and
　　　　　　　　　　　　　　　　　　　　　　　　～を救う
train himself.
～を鍛える

⑨As he returns to the common people he had once left and
　　　　　　　　　　　　　一般の(→世俗の)

118

continues to train himself, he will attain the real enlightenment.

47. 竿頭進歩(かんとうしんぽ)(『無門関』四十六則)

①石霜(せきそう)和尚は「百尺(ひゃくしゃく)の竿(さお)の頂点で、どうやってそこから一歩を進めることができるのか」と問いました。
②また、別の昔の和尚は、「百尺の竿の頂点にずっと坐(すわ)っている人は、道を究(きわ)めたといっても本物とはいえない。③竿の頂上からさらに一歩踏み出せば、あらゆる方向、あらゆる世界で自分のすべての能力を発揮することができる」と言いました。
④百尺の竿の頂点とは、修行を積んでのぼり詰めた悟りの境地を象徴しています。
⑤禅の悟りの境地に到達しても、そこで気を抜いてしまうと、執着心が起きます。
⑥悟りを開いた後からが大切です。⑦竿の先端から飛翔(ひしょう)するのです。⑧そして、世俗(せぞく)におりて、皆を救いながら自らも再び修行をするのです。
⑨一度捨てた世俗の人々の間に戻り、自分をさらに磨き続けることで、真の悟りに至るのです。

48 Master *Baso* Is Ill

①When Master *Baso* was seriously ill, the chief inspector of the temple came to see him and asked him, "Master, how are you feeling these days?"

②The Master answered; "Sun-face Buddha, Moon-face Buddha."

③Sun-face Buddha is the fifty-eighth Buddha among one thousand Buddhas in the present world and has a long life of 1800 years.

④Moon-face Buddha, 202nd Buddha in the present world, has a short life of one day and one night long.

⑤Master *Baso*, being asked about the condition of his health, answered with the names of these two Buddhas.

⑥The contrast between the Buddha of the longest life and of the shortest life reminds us to abandon a relative concept.

⑦One day is the same length for Sun-face Buddha and Moon-face Buddha.

第5章 「公案」を読む

⑧His words mean that, whether life is as short as only one
　　　　　　　　　　　　　　たとえ〜でも―でも
day or is immeasurably long, it is life that is significant.
　　　計り知れないほどの　　　　　　　　　意義のあるもの
⑨This is a stage of enlightenment where he does not mind

whether he continues to live or dies soon.

---

48. 馬大師不安（『碧巌録』三則）

①馬祖禅師が重い病に苦しんでいたので、院主が見舞いに来て、「和尚さま、近ごろの具合はいかがですか？」と尋ねました。
②「日面仏と、月面仏だ」と師は答えました。
③「日面仏」とは、現世において出世される千人の仏様の第58番目の仏で、1800歳という長寿の仏です。
④「月面仏」は第202番目の仏で、一日一夜という寿命の短い仏です。
⑤馬祖は具合を尋ねられたときの返事で、その二つの仏の名を出しています。
⑥両極端の寿命を持つ仏の名を挙げて、相対的な観念から抜け出しなさいということです。
⑦「日面仏」の一日も、「月面仏」の一日も、同じ一日です。
⑧一晩で死のうと、気の遠くなるくらい長生きしようと、どちらも価値のある一生に違いないことを表しています。
⑨「生きるのもよし、死ぬのもよし」といった悟りの境地です。

49 *Tōzan's* "Cold and Heat"

①This is a conversation between a priest and Master *Tōzan*, the founder of the Chinese *Sōtō* school.
②The priest said to the master, "I'm suffering from the heat and the cold. ③How can I escape from this suffering?"
④"Then you should go to the place where heat and cold do not exist", the master answered.
⑤The priest again asked the master, "What kind of place is it where heat and cold do not exist?" ⑥The master replied, "You should just be cold when you feel cold and just be hot when you feel heat."

⑦What the master means is that it is important to assimilate yourself into the heat when you feel hot and to assimilate yourself into the cold when you feel cold.

⑧The heat and cold are metaphors for suffering in life.
⑨You can transcend the suffering in life by opposing the suffering positively, removing the wall between the

suffering and yourself and assimilating yourself into the suffering.

⑩ This is one of the ultimate states of Zen.
　　　　　　　　　　　　　　　　境地

---

49. 洞山無寒暑(とうざんむかんじょ)(『碧巌録』四十三則)

① 中国の曹洞宗の開祖である洞山禅師とある僧の会話です。
② その僧が洞山禅師に「寒さや暑さで苦しい思いをしています。
③ どうしたらこの苦しみを避けることができますか」と尋ねました。④「寒さや暑さのない場所にいけばいいのだ」と禅師は答えました。
⑤ さらに、僧は聞きました。「寒さや暑さのない場所とはどんなところですか」⑥「寒いときは寒さになりきり、暑いときは暑さになりきるのだ」と洞山禅師は答えました。
⑦ 寒さや暑さから逃避(とうひ)せずに、寒いときには寒さと、暑いときには暑さと同化することが大切だと禅師は言っています。
⑧ 寒さや暑さは、人生の苦悩のたとえです。
⑨ 苦悩と積極的に向かい合い、苦悩と自分との境界を取り払い、一体化することにより、苦悩を超越することができるということです。
⑩ これも禅の境地の一つです。

50 Not the Wind, Not the Flag

①Two priests were arguing about a flag flapping in the wind.

②One said: "The flag is moving." ③The other said: "The wind is moving."

④They kept insisting.

⑤The sixth patriarch *Eno* happened to see it and told them: "Not the wind, not the flag; your mind is moving."

⑥The two priests were frightened to hear this.

⑦They hold fast to objects such as the flag and wind. ⑧*Eno* told them that the mind is moving in order for the priests to cease holding onto objects.

⑨The wind, the flag, and the mind existed as it was just independently. ⑩They are not related. ⑪There is no distinction or "*Funbetsu*" between the things in the Zen world. ⑫The purpose of Zen training, in which trainees solve *kōans*, is to feel it as reality.

第5章 「公案」を読む

50. 非風非幡(ひふうひばん)（『無門関』二十九則）

①二人の僧が寺の前で、風でパタパタ揺れている幡(はた)を見て言い争っていました。
②一人は「幡が動いている」と言います。③もう一人は「いや風が動いているのだ」と言います。
④お互いに言い張って譲(ゆず)りません。
⑤それを見た六祖の慧能(えのう)が、「風が動くのでも、幡が動くのでもない。あなたたちの心が動いているのだ」と言いました。
⑥二人の僧は、それを聞いて恐れおののきました。
⑦僧たちは、風と幡という物に囚(とら)われ執着しています。⑧慧能が「心が動いている」と言ったのは、その物への執着を捨てさせるためです。
⑨風と幡と心が、あるがままにあります。⑩対立しているのではありません。⑪禅の世界には分別(ふんべつ)はないのです。⑫これを実感としてとらえるのが、公案を解く修行です。

51　*Keichū* Makes a Cart

①Master *Gettan* asked a priest:
"*Keichū* made one hundred carts, but he removed not only the wheels but also the axles. ②What was he going to do?"
③*Keichū* is thought to be the first wheel-maker of ancient China, the *Xia* Dynasty.
④Why did *Keichū* disassemble all the carts which he had made after all his hard work?
⑤When the parts are taken off from the cart, it is not a cart any more, although they once formed a cart.
⑥If you think of the parts of the cart as body parts, these separate parts of the body might not have the substance of your own body.

⑦Using the metaphor of *Keichū's* cart, Master *Gettan* tried to find what the self is.
⑧Where is the substance of the self?

⑨ It is nowhere; it is attributed to "*mu*".

51. 奚仲造車（『無門関』八則）

①月庵和尚がある僧に尋ねました。「奚仲は、百台も車を造ったのだけれども、彼はその両輪を外し、車軸もとってしまった。
②何を明らかにしようとしたのか」
③奚仲は古代中国の夏王朝で車を発明したとされる人物です。
④その奚仲が、せっかく造った車をバラバラにするということは、何を象徴しているのでしょうか。
⑤解体した部品の一つひとつは、車を構成していましたが、それ自体は車ではありません。
⑥車を、自分に置き換えてみると、身体の部分部分には自分としての実体があるとはいえません。
⑦月庵和尚は、奚仲の車のエピソードにたとえて、自己を摸索するという試みをしていたのです。
⑧人間の実体とはどこにあるのでしょうか。
⑨どこにもない、「無」に行き着くという解釈です。

52 The Sound of One Hand

①This *kōan* asks: "If you clap with only one hand, what does it sound like?".

②This is a *kōan* composed in Japan by *Hakuin* who is said to be the founder of the Japan *Rinzai* school. ③This is the first barrier for trainees of the *Rinzai* school.

④If you clap with two hands, it sounds like "clap". ⑤You can not make a sound with one hand. ⑥The trainees who stick to common sense and logic have difficulty answering. ⑦*Hakuin* intended for trainees to throw out common sense. ⑧In order to separate from the preconception that you hear the sound with ears and in order to hear the sound with the mind, you need to be released from the bounds of common sense.

⑨It is said that *Suzuki Daisetsu* clapped his hands and asked the audience if it was the right hand or the left hand that made the sound, when he gave lectures in Europe and

the United States. ⑩It seems to be a excellent way in which
　　　　　　　　　　　　　すばらしい　　　　　そこでは〜する
to spread the ideology of Zen.
広める　イデオロギー

---

52. 隻手音声(せきしゅおんじょう)(『白隠禅師坐禅和讃(はくいんぜんじざぜんわさん)』)

①隻手音声の公案は「片手で拍手すると、どんな音がするのか？」というものです。

②これは、日本の臨済宗を興(おこ)したとされる白隠（p170参照）によってつくられた日本製の公案です。③臨済宗の参禅者にとって、この公案が最初の関門になります。

④両手を叩(たた)けばパンという音が出ます。⑤片手では音を出すことはできません。⑥常識や理屈に囚われている人は、答えに窮(きゅう)してしまいます。

⑦白隠の狙(ねら)いは、常識を捨てさせることにあります。⑧耳で音を聞くという思い込みから離れて、心で音を聞くためには、常識という束縛から逃れる必要があるからです。

⑨鈴木大拙（p174参照）が、欧米での講演のとき、大勢の聴衆の前で拍手を打って、その音は右手から出た音か左手から出た音かを尋ねたといいます。⑩禅の思想を広めるための見事なパフォーマンスではなかったでしょうか。

People Influenced by Zen / 禅の影響を受けた人々④

Natsume Sōseki 　　　　夏目 漱石
　　　　　　　　　　　　　なつ め　そう せき

Natsume Sōseki was a Japanese leading novelist during the *Meiji* to *Taisho* periods. In some scenes of his novels, such as "*Mon*" or "The Gate", he described zazen practices. It is known that *Sōseki*, at the age of twenty-seven, practiced zazen at *Enkaku-ji* temple, located in *Kamakura*. Although he did not practice zazen many times, Zen influenced his works particularly the theme of conflict between "self" and one's surroundings.

In his later years, he arrived at the idea of "*sokuten kyoshi*" which means "following heaven and abandoning self". This phrase, "*sokuten kyoshi*", is thought to share common ideas with Zen.

夏目漱石は、明治から大正時代の日本を代表する小説家です。漱石は、『門』などいくつかの小説で、坐禅をする場面を描きました。27歳のとき、鎌倉の円覚寺で数日間坐禅したことが知られています。坐禅の体験はほんの数日ですが、禅は自己と社会や周囲の人間との葛藤を描く漱石の小説に影響を与えました。

晩年、漱石は『則天去私』という考えに至りました。これは「自己を捨てて天に従う」ことを意味します。この言葉は禅に通じるものがあるとされています。

Chapter 6

Zen's Words

....

第6章

禅のことば

Zen Buddhism

53 Communication Without Words, a Lesson Without Teaching

①The origin of these phrases are from the story of the Flower Sermon (see p.34).
②Some of Buddha's teachings cannot be expressed in words. ③Those should be taught with neither words nor sutras. ④The teachings of Zen are communicated from a master to a disciple face to face: this method is called "*menju shihou*".
⑤The disciple should take the teaching from the bowl of the master without missing a drop; this is called "*shishi sosho*".

⑥A trainee priest searches for the truth through the same experiences of zazen as Buddha. ⑦After polishing the mind with zazen, he can see what cannot be described. ⑧The master, examining the action of the disciple and his response to the *kōan*, judges if he understands the teaching

or not. ⑨The master's approval is called "*inka*", and disciples approved by the master are called "*hossu*".
認定　　　　　　　　　　　印可
　　　　　　　　　　　　　　　　　　　　　　法嗣

53. 不立文字と教外別伝
　　　ふ りゅうもん じ　きょう げ べつでん

①これらの言葉の起源は、「拈華微笑（p34参照）」のエピソードです。
　　　　　　　　　　　　　ねん げ み しょう

②釈迦の教えの中には、文字で伝えることができないものもあります（不立文字）。③それらは、文字や言葉や経典に頼らずに伝えるしかありません（教外別伝）。④禅の教えは、師から弟子に、面と向かって直接関わって伝えるという「面授嗣法」というやり方で伝えられます。
　　　　　　　　　　　　　　　　　　　　　　めんじゅ し ほう

⑤教えを、師の器から一滴ももらさずに受けなければなりません。これを「師資相承」といいます。
　　　　　　し し そうしょう

⑥修行者は坐禅という釈迦の追体験をして真理を探ります。
　　　　　　　　　　　　　　　　　　　　　　さぐ

⑦坐禅によって心と智慧を磨くと、文字に表せないことも理解できるようになります。⑧師は弟子の行動や公案の返答を見て弟子が教えを理解したかどうかを確かめます。⑨師が認めることを印可といい、印可を受けた弟子を法嗣と呼びます。
　　いん か　　　　　　　　　　　　　　　　　はっ す

54 Seize Your "Mind of Buddha", Be Aware of Your "Mind of Buddha"

①"*Jikishi ninshin*" is a phrase which means you should firmly seize the "mind of Buddha" that is deep in your own mind. ②This can be possible when you look closely inside of yourself.

③If you are searching for something outside of yourself, you will have difficulty or suffering.

④"*Kensho jobutsu*" means that you should be aware of your own "mind of Buddha" and become a Buddha.

⑤Essentially all of us have Buddha inside of us.

⑥The true meaning of the words, "To become a Buddha", is to be aware of the Buddha inside of you, even though it means death in Japanese.

⑦Enlightenment is to be aware of the pure nature of yourself as Buddha.

⑧Zen is practice to realize the mind of Buddha within

yourself, and to return to the nature of yourself.

54. 直指人心 と見性成仏
<small>じきしにんしん　けんしょうじょうぶつ</small>

①「直指人心」とは、自分の心の奥深くにある仏心を、しっかりつかみ取りなさいという意味の言葉です。
②そのためには、自分の内面をよく見なければなりません。
③外側に何かを求めると、迷いや苦悩の原因になります。
④「見性成仏」とは、自分の仏心をしっかりと自覚して、仏になりなさいという意味です。
⑤私たち一人ひとりの中にもともと仏がいます。
⑥「成仏」とは、一般には死ぬことを指していますが、本当の意味は、「仏になる」、つまり自覚した人間になるという意味です。
⑦悟りとは、本来の純粋な自分が仏であることを自覚するということです。
⑧すでに備わっている仏心を確認し、本来の自分に戻ることが、禅なのです。

55　Hero

①This is a word that comes from chapter twelve of The Gateless Gate.
『無門関』

②Master *Zuigan*, a Zen priest in the *Tang* Dynasty, called out to himself "Hero!" and answered "Yes!"
瑞巌　　　　　　　　　　唐時代　　　　　　　　　　　主人公！

③Then he continued: "Do you wake up well?"

"Yes."

"Don't be cheated."
騙される

"Yes."

④He talked to himself in a loud voice every day.
　　独り言を言った　大きな声で

⑤When you are stimulated by the environment, you become out of control, and being swayed by the illusion, you lose yourself.
刺激を受ける　周囲から　コントロールできない　~することによって　妄想でふくれる(→妄想に惑わされる)

⑥Master *Zuigan* made himself aware of his individuality by speaking to himself.
自分を目覚めさせる　主体性

136

⑦Hero is the unity of the self who talks to and the self who
　　　　　　　統一
answers.

⑧If you are the hero of your world, you can live freely,
　　　　　　　　　　　　　　　　　　　　　　　　　自由に生きる
being bound by nothing.
何にも束縛されずに

55. 主人公

①『無門関』の十二則に使われている言葉です。
②唐時代の禅僧・瑞巌和尚は、毎日自分自身に向かって、「主人公！」と呼びかけ、また自分で「はい」と返事をしていました。
③「はっきりと目を醒ましているか」、「はい」。「これからも人に騙されてはいけないよ」、「はい」。
④和尚は毎日大きな声で独り言を言っていました。
⑤人は周囲からさまざまな刺激を受けると、自分をコントロールすることができなくなり、妄想に惑わされて自分を見失います。
⑥この和尚は、自分に話しかけることによって主体性を目覚めさせていたのです。
⑦「問う自己」と「答える自己」が一体化したものが主人公です。
⑧自分が自分の世界の主人公でいれば、すべてのものに束縛されず、自由に生きていくことができます。

56   Wrestle in Sitting

①*Dōgen* (see p.160) preached in his book that the most important training was to devote yourself to sitting as the Buddha did.

②This is "wrestle in sitting".

③*Dōgen* criticized the idea of practicing zazen to attain enlightenment. ④He also criticized the idea that training was not necessary because everyone naturally had the "nature of Buddha".

⑤Therefore the purpose of "wrestle in sitting" is not to attain enlightenment.

⑥It is just sitting with thinking of nothing and having no purpose. ⑦*Dōgen* wrote that the aspect of sitting is the aspect of enlightenment.

⑧Practicing zazen lets the mind and body be free from everything. ⑨As a result the mind separates from the body, and then you might see the world of enlightenment.

第6章 禅のことば

⑩ According to *Dōgen*, enlightenment is in continuous
　　～によれば　　　　　　　　　　　　　　　　　　　連続的な
sitting, and you should continue to sit after attaining enlightenment.

---

56. 只管打坐(しかんたざ)

①道元（p160参照）は自著の中で、釈迦と同じようにただひたすら坐禅をすることが一番大事であると説いています。
②これが「只管打坐」です。
③道元は、悟りを得るために坐禅を組むという考え方を批判しました。④同時に、人は生まれながらにして仏心を持つので、修行は必要ないという考え方も批判しました。
⑤したがって、只管打坐は、悟りを得るために坐り続けることではありません。
⑥何の目的も持たず、何も考えずにひたすら坐り続けるのです。
⑦その坐り続けている姿こそ、悟りの姿だと道元は書いています。
⑧坐禅を続けるうちに、身も心も一切の束縛から逃(のが)れられます。
⑨そして、「身心脱落(しんじんだつらく)」の状態になり、周囲に悟りの世界が開けるのです。
⑩坐り続けることこそ悟りであり、悟りに至っても、さらに坐り続けるのです。

139

57　*Samadhi* of One Practice

①The Japanese word "*zanmai*" means devotion to a particular thing.

②The origin of this Japanese word, *Samadhi*, is a Sanskrit word, originating from Indian meditation.

③The essence of Zen training is to concentrate on zazen.

④The sixth patriarch *Eno*, described in his work, "Platform Sutra" as follows:

⑤"*Samadhi* of One Practice" is to do everything with a pure mind, not having any illusions and redundant ideas; in actions such as walking, stopping, sitting and sleeping.

⑥Zen training is not only practicing zazen.

⑦Each action of daily life

can be training if you decisively concentrate on it with a
断固として(→徹底的に)

pure mind.

⑧It is a true practice of Buddhism when you always stay in this stage of *Samadhi*.
境地

57. 一行三昧 (いちぎょうざんまい)

①「三昧」とは一つの物事に打ち込むことを意味します。
②この言葉の語源となったサンスクリット語のサマディは、インドの瞑想(めいそう)から生まれた言葉です。
③禅の修行では、坐禅に集中することが基本です。
④六祖の慧能(えのう)は、著作『六祖壇経(ろくそだんきょう)』の中で、次のように述べています。
⑤「行(ぎょう)(歩くこと)、住(じゅう)(立ち止まること)、坐(ざ)(坐ること)、臥(が)(寝ること)という行動において、常に純粋な心で雑念も妄想もいだくことなく、物事にあたることが一行三昧である」。
⑥禅の修行は坐禅を組むだけではありません。⑦一つひとつの行ないにも純粋な心で、徹底的に集中することで、日常生活が禅修行の道場になります。⑧常にこの三昧の境地にいることこそ、正しい仏道を歩んでいることになるのです。

58 Let It Go

①The word "*hōgejaku*" means "let it go".

②*Gen-yō*, a Zen priest of the *Táng* Dynasty, attained enlightenment when he stripped everything away and became pure self.

③Then he asked *Joshū*: "I stripped everything away and I have nothing now. ④What should I do from now?"

⑤*Joshū* replied: "*Hōgejaku* (Just let it go!)"

⑥*Gen-yō* asked again: "I reached a stage of nothingness and I have nothing. ⑦What should I let go?"

⑧*Joshū* replied: "If you say so, then bring it all back home."

⑨*Joshū* told *Gen-yō* to abandon his mind of holding fast to nothingness and even abandon the action where he had stripped everything away.

⑩This means, you must not hold fast even to enlightenment.

第6章　禅のことば

趙州和尚

58. 放下著（ほうげじゃく）

①「放下著」とは「捨ててしまえ」という意味です。
②中国の唐の時代、厳陽（げんよう）という僧は、何もかも捨てて「無一物（むいちぶつ）」という純粋な自己になり、悟りを開きました。
③そして厳陽は、名僧の趙州（じょうしゅう）に尋ねました。「何もかも捨て去って、一物も持っておりません。④これから先はどうしたらいいのでしょうか」
⑤この問いに対して、趙州は「放下著（捨ててしまえ）」と一言。
⑥厳陽：「私は、無の境地に至り、何も持っておりませんが。⑦一体全体、何を捨てるのでしょうか」
⑧趙州：「それほど言うなら、すべてを担（かつ）いで帰りなさい」
⑨趙州は、厳陽の捨てたことに対するこだわりと無に対する執着を捨てろと言ったのです。
⑩「悟ったこと」にも執着してはならないということです。

59. A Day Without Work, Is a Day Without Eating

①This teaching says: "If you spend a day without working at training, you must not eat that day."

②*Hyakujō Ekai* is a Zen priest from the *Tang* Dynasty who established rules on training and labor in Zen temples. ③Since economic activity of priests having been forbidden in Buddhism in this period, most of the priests could not live on offerings and begging. ④*Hyakujō*, believed labor to be a part of training, and lived off the land. ⑤He toiled long hours on the farm everyday until he was over the age of 90 years.

⑥One day a disciple, concerned about his health, hid his farm tools and asked him to take a rest. ⑦*Hyakujō* looked for his tools, but could not find them. ⑧Then he said "A day without work, is a day without eating" and didn't eat his meal that day. ⑨After this, the disciples never stopped his

第6章　禅のことば

labor.

⑩ Therefore, labor, such as farming and chopping firewood
　そのため　　　　　　　　　　　　　　耕作すること　　薪を割ること
was thought to be a part of training for Zen priests.

---

59. 一日不作一日不食 (いちじつなさざれば　いちじつくらわず)

①「修行である労働が一日できないのならば、食べることもできない」という教えです。
②百丈懐海(ひゃくじょうえかい)は、禅寺の労働や修行生活の規則をつくった唐時代の禅僧です。
③当時、仏教では、僧侶の経済活動を認めなかったので、僧侶は布施(ふせ)や托鉢(たくはつ)だけでは生活をまかなえませんでした。④百丈は労働も修行の一つであるとし、田畑での自給自足を行ないました。⑤百丈は、自ら90歳をすぎても毎日農作業に精を出していました。
⑥ある日、百丈の体調を案じた弟子が道具を隠し、禅師に休むように頼みました。⑦百丈は道具を探しましたが、見つかりませんでした。⑧そして百丈は「一日作さざれば一日食らわず」と言って食事をとろうとしませんでした。⑨このことがあってから、弟子たちは師の労働を止めることはしませんでした。
⑩このようにして、禅僧にとって畑を耕(たがや)したり、薪(まき)を割ったりして汗を流して働くことが、修行の一部と考えられるようになりました。

60　Everyday Is a Good Day

①This Zen phrase just means everyday is good.
②At the end of the *Tang* Dynasty, a Zen priest *Unmon* told his disciple; ③"I don't care about your past. ④What will be your future? ⑤Make a phrase of it."
⑥None of them could make one, so he made the phrase "Everyday is a good day" as an example.

⑦Days are not always fine in your life. ⑧They are sometimes rainy or stormy or else sad or disappointing. ⑨To feel that everyday is good, you should live just as well as possible in every moment. ⑩No matter what the circumstances, you should find something beautiful, right or good. ⑪If you find these wonderful things in your heart, everyday becomes a good day.

⑫You should feel that your life is only one day, that day.

⑬Spending days in this way, your life will be satisfied.

60. 日日是好日(にちにちこれこうじつ)

①この禅語は、「毎日毎日がよい日ばかりだ」という意味です。
②唐代の末期にいた禅僧の雲門(うんもん)が弟子たちにこう言いました。
③「いままでの日々のことは、問わない。④これからはどうなのか。⑤一句にしてみよ」
⑥誰もつくることができなかったので、雲門は自分で「日日是好日」という一句を参考につくって見せました。
⑦人生は、晴れた日ばかりではありません。⑧嵐の日や、疲れた日や、絶望した日など、いろいろな日があります。⑨そうした毎日を、いつもよい日と感じていくには、瞬間瞬間を精一杯生きるということに尽きます。⑩どんな状況のときも、美しいもの、正しいこと、よいものを見つけることです。⑪そのすばらしさを心で受け止めることができれば、毎日はよい日になります。
⑫自分の人生は今日一日しかないと思って、その日一日を充実させていく。⑬そうした日々を積み重ねていくことで、充実した人生になるということです。

61 The True Face

① The Japanese word "*honrai no menmoku*" is the true face or mind which everyone naturally has. ② This word derives from a story about *Eno* (see p.42), the sixth patriarch of Chinese Zen.

③ *Eno*, selected for the sixth patriarch in competition with a senior disciple, left the temple to travel. ④ One of his fellow priests, *Emyo*, envied him and chased him to seize a robe and a bowl, the symbols of the patriarch.
⑤ *Eno* said to *Emyo*: "What is your true face, if you do not think this is good nor do you think this is evil?"
⑥ At the moment, *Emyo* attained great enlightenment.
⑦ *Emyo*, sweating from all the pores of his body and groveling, asked *Eno* again: "⑧ How can I find a deeper part of the secret you gave me?"

⑨ *Eno* replied: "What I told you right now is not secret.
⑩ Once you have realized your true face, the secret rather

148

belongs to you!"
　むしろあなたにある

⑪The true face everyone naturally has is hidden, being
　　　　　　　　　　　　　　　　　　　　　隠れている
covered with emotions, desires and obsessions. ⑫The true
　　　　　　　　感情　　　　欲望　　　　　執着心
face will appear when we strip these things off.
　　　　現れる　　　　　　　　〜を捨て去る

61. 本来の面目（ほんらい　めんもく）

①「本来の面目」とは、人がもともと持っているありのままの心性を表しています。②この言葉の由来は、中国禅六祖・慧能（えのう）のエピソードにあります（p42参照）。

③慧能は、兄弟子をさし置いて六祖に選ばれると、寺をあとにして旅に出ました。④これをねたむ兄弟子の慧明（えみょう）は、六祖の証（あかし）である衣鉢（いはつ）を奪おうと、慧能を追いました。⑤慧能は、慧明に向かってこう言いました。「善をも悪をも思わない、あなたの本来の面目は一体何なのか？」⑥これを聞いた慧明は悟りを開きました。⑦全身から汗が噴出し、這（は）いつくばった慧明は、再び慧能に尋ねました。⑧「今教えていただいた秘密を、さらに深めるためには、どうしたらいいのでしょうか？」⑨慧能は、「これは秘密ではない。⑩あなたが自分自身の面目で照らせば、秘密はあなたの中にあるのです」と答えました。

⑪誰でも感情、欲望、執着心があるので、本来持っている心性が隠されてしまいます。⑫それらを捨て去ったときに、現れてくるのが本来の面目ということです。

62 Have a Cup of Tea

① The word "*kissako*", which derives from a *kōan*, "The Quotations from *Joshū*", means "have a cup of tea".

② The story of the *kōan* is as follows.

③ One day a priest came to see *Joshū* and to listen to his lecture.

④ *Joshū* asked: "Have you ever been here before?"

The priest answered: "Yes I have."

Joshū said: "Have a cup of tea."

⑤ A different time, another priest came.

⑥ *Joshū* asked: "Have you ever been here before?"

The priest answered: "No, I haven't."

Joshū said: "Have a cup of tea."

⑦ Since *Joshū* repeated this phrase to all the visitors, the chief of the temple asked: "Why did you offer tea to everyone?" ⑧ *Joshū* just replied: "Have a cup of tea."

⑨ Though there are various interpretations of this *kōan*, the

第6章　禅のことば

most common among them is that "the important thing is offering a cup of tea to everyone impartially without any discrimination of status". ⑩Since this word is loved by people who practice tea ceremony, we often see the scroll calligraphy of this word in tea ceremony rooms.
　提供すること　　　　　　　　公平に
　区別　　　　　　地位(身分)
　　　　　　　　　　茶道
　　　　　　　　　　　　　　　　掛け軸の書(墨蹟)
　　　　　　　　　　　　　　茶室

62. 喫茶去(きっさこ)

①「喫茶去」は『趙州録(じょうしゅうろく)』にある公案で、「一杯のお茶を飲みなさい」という意味です。②この公案は次のような内容です。
③趙州のところにある僧が教えを請(こ)いに来ました。
④趙州:「あんたはここに来たことがあったかい?」僧:「はい、あります」趙州:「まあ、お茶でも飲みなさい」
⑤またあるとき、別の僧がやって来ました。
⑥趙州:「あんたはここに来たことがあったかい?」僧:「いいえ、ありません」趙州:「まあ、お茶でも飲みなさい」
⑦趙州が、すべての訪問者にこのように問うので、院主は「どうして、ここに来たことがある人にも、ない人にも、お茶を飲みなさいと勧(すす)めるのですか」と聞きました。⑧「おい、院主さん。まあ、お茶でも飲みなさい」と趙州は答えました。
⑨この公案にはさまざまな解釈がありますが、中でも一番一般的なのは、「分別(ふんべつ)や偏見(へんけん)を持たずに、どのような身分の人にも、差別することなく茶を勧めることが大切だ」ということです。⑩この言葉は、茶道愛好家に親しまれており、茶室で墨蹟(ぼくせき)をよく見かけます。

151

63. The Neutral Mind Is the Way

①"*Byo jo shin kore dou*", in Japanese, or "the neutral mind is the way" is a phrase from *Baso*, a Chinese Zen master of the *Tang* Dynasty.

②He preached as follows: "If you want to find the way directly, the neutral mind is the way. ③Well, what is the neutral mind? ④Don't think about anything, don't agree or refuse, don't make choices, don't stop or continue, don't be ordinary or great."

⑤And he continued; "Now you are going, coming back, sitting and lying down and also taking action aligning yourself with other people. ⑥All of these are the way."

⑦Therefore "neutral mind" of "the neutral mind is the way" means neither "calm" nor "ordinary".

⑧Living naturally with the honest mind you are born with lets you find your way to practice the truth.

63. 平常心是道
びょうじょうしんこれどう

① 「平常心是道」は唐代の禅僧馬祖の言葉です。
② 馬祖は、次のように説きました。「もしあなたが、直に道を見つけたければ、平常心こそ道だ。③ 平常心とは何であろうか？
④ 何も考えず、同意もしなければ拒否もしない、選択もしない、止めたり続けたりしない、凡庸にも偉大にもならない、ということだ」
⑤ 彼は続けてこう言いました。「誰でも行き来したり、坐ったり寝転んだり、他人に合わせた行動をとったりしている。⑥ こうしたことすべてが道なのだ」
⑦ したがって「平常心是道」といったときの「平常心」は、「穏やかなで日常的な心」という意味ではありません。
⑧ 「生まれながらに持ち合わせている素直な心で、あるがままに暮らすことが、真実を実践する道へとあなたを導く」という意味です。

64 Desire Little and Know Contentment

①The translation of the phrase "*shoyoku chisoku*" is "desire little and know contentment".

②Eight key phrases to be enlightened are explained in "The Eight Lessons to be a Great Man", the last preaching of the Buddha. ③The phrases in "the Eight Lessons to be a Great Man" are as follows.

④Desiring little. ⑤Knowing contentment. ⑥Enjoying silence and loneliness. ⑦Devoting yourself. ⑧Keeping awareness. ⑨Acquiring *dhyaana* (concentrating on objects and searching for the truth). ⑩Cultivating wisdom. ⑪Not being wordy.

⑫"Desire little and know contentment" is a combination of "desiring little" and "knowing contentment", these two phrases concerning desire rank at the top of the eight phrases. ⑬Even for modern people, desire can be the cause of agony. ⑭We should remember this phrase which means

第6章 禅のことば

"your mind will be rich if you control your desire and learn to feel contentment."

五知円(ごちえん)：京都の龍安寺などにあるつくばいには、「五隹止矢」の4文字が刻まれています。真ん中の四角い部分が「口」を表し、それぞれを部首として加えると「吾唯足知」（われただたることをしる）となります。

64. 少欲知足（しょうよくちそく）

①少欲知足とは、欲望を少なくし、満足を知るという意味です。②釈迦の最後の説法である「八大人覚（はちだいにんがく）」には、悟りにいたるための八つのキーワードが説かれています。③「八大人覚」にあるそれらの言葉は、次のとおりです。

④少欲（しょうよく）（多くを欲しない）、⑤知足（ちそく）（満足することを知る）、⑥楽寂静（ぎょうじゃくじょう）（静寂を楽しむ）、⑦勤精進（ごんしょうじん）（すべてに励（はげ）む）、⑧不忘念（ふもうねん）（ひたむきに思うことを忘れない）、⑨修禅定（しゅぜんじょう）（心を集中して真実を探（さぐ）る）、⑩修智慧（しゅちえ）（智慧を身につける）、⑪不戯論（ふけろん）（無駄な議論をしない）です。

⑫少欲知足は、八つあるうちの冒頭にある、欲望に関係する二つの言葉、「少欲」と「知足」を組み合わせたものです。⑬現代人にとっても欲望は苦しみの原因になります。⑭「欲望を抑え、満足を知れば、心が豊かになる」という、この言葉の意味を、私たちはぜひ覚えておきたいものです。

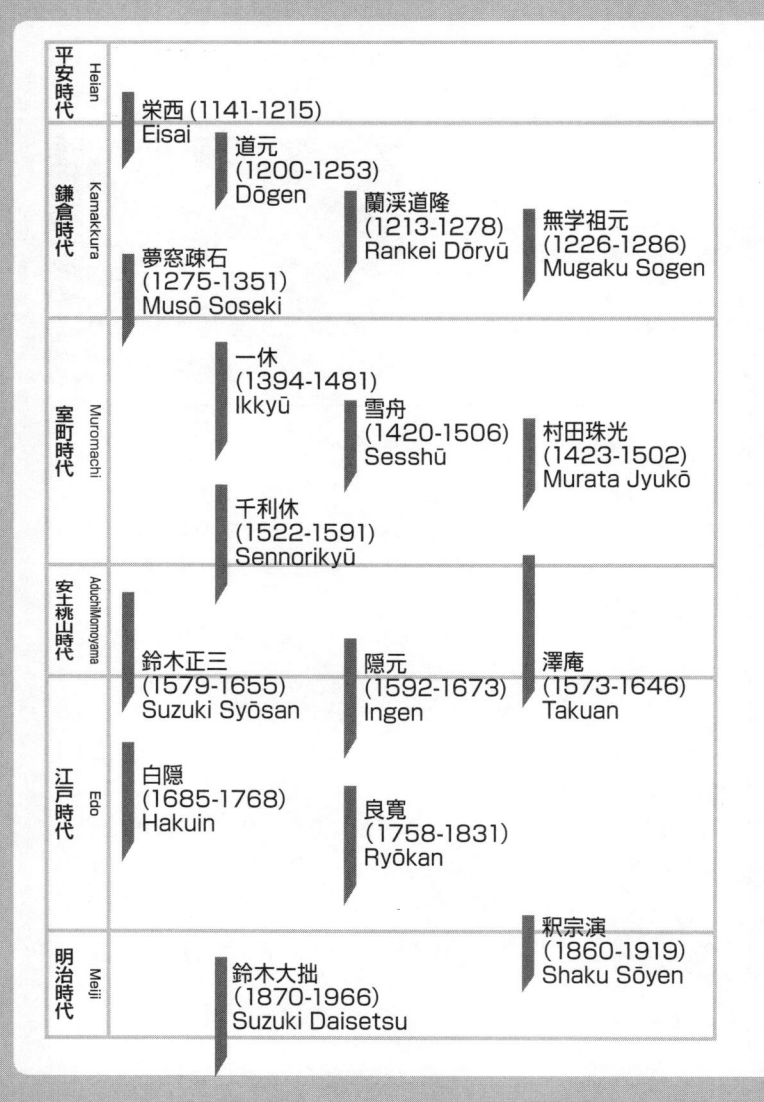

Japanese Zen Masters Chronology / 日本禅師年表

平安時代 / Heian	栄西 (1141-1215) Eisai
鎌倉時代 / Kamakkura	道元 (1200-1253) Dōgen 蘭渓道隆 (1213-1278) Rankei Dōryū 無学祖元 (1226-1286) Mugaku Sogen 夢窓疎石 (1275-1351) Musō Soseki
室町時代 / Muromachi	一休 (1394-1481) Ikkyū 雪舟 (1420-1506) Sesshū 村田珠光 (1423-1502) Murata Jyukō 千利休 (1522-1591) Sennorikyū
安土桃山時代 / AduchiMomoyama	
江戸時代 / Edo	鈴木正三 (1579-1655) Suzuki Syōsan 隠元 (1592-1673) Ingen 澤庵 (1573-1646) Takuan 白隠 (1685-1768) Hakuin 良寛 (1758-1831) Ryōkan
明治時代 / Meiji	釈宗演 (1860-1919) Shaku Sōyen 鈴木大拙 (1870-1966) Suzuki Daisetsu

156

Chapter 7

Profile of Zen Masters

第 7 章
禅師たちのプロフィール

Zen Buddhism

65   *Myōan Eisai*

①*Myōan Eisai* is a priest who brought the *Rinzai* school from China to Japan. ②He became a priest of the *Tendai* school at the Mt.*Hiei Enryaku-ji* temple when he was fourteen years old.

③After studying Buddhism for more than ten years, *Eisai* was disappointed with Japanese Buddhism and decided to go to China to learn orthodox Buddhism. ④Although it was not easy to travel by boat to China at that time, *Eisai* visited there twice. ⑤For the first trip in 1168, he visited *Ashoka*-Temple where he came across Zen Buddhism. ⑥In 1187, *Eisai* left Japan again to go to India. ⑦When he arrived at China, he realized that the route to India was not safe. ⑧He decided not to go to India and stayed in China for four years as a disciple of ō *Eshō*, a master of the *Rinzai* school. ⑨After his certification as a Zen teacher, *Eisai* returned to Japan in 1191, bringing Zen scriptures and tea

seeds.
種
⑩Therefore he is known as the priest to introduce the
　　　　　　　　　　　　　　　　　　　　　　　　　広める
custom of drinking tea as well as the priest to bring the
習慣　　　　　　　　　　〜であるとともに　　　　　　　伝えた
Rinzai school of Zen to Japan.

---

65. 栄西 (1141~1215)

①明菴栄西は、中国から日本に臨済宗をもたらしました。②栄西は、14歳で比叡山の延暦寺で天台密教の僧侶になりました。③10年以上仏教を修めた栄西でしたが、日本の仏教に失望して中国で正統的な仏教を学ぼうと決心しました。④当時、中国に船で渡るのは容易なことではありませんでしたが、栄西は2度訪れています。⑤1168年に、栄西が最初の渡航をしたときに訪れた阿育王寺で、禅宗に出会いました。⑥栄西は1187年に日本から再び出てインドに向かいました。⑦中国に着いた栄西は、インドまでのルートが安全ではないことを知りました。⑧インドに行くことを断念して中国に滞在し、臨済宗の指導者である虚庵懐敞に4年間師事しました。⑨禅師としての印可状を受けた栄西は、1191年に日本に禅の経典と茶の種を携えて戻りました。

⑩日本では、栄西は臨済宗を伝えた僧であるとともに、喫茶の習慣を広めた人物として知られています。

66   *Dōgen*

①Seeing the death of his mother at a very young age, *Dōgen* entered the Mt.*Hiei Enryaku-ji* temple of the *Tendai* school to become a priest. ②According to the teaching of the *Tendai* school, it is said that everyone has the mind of Buddha by nature. ③*Dōgen* wondered why a priest should train even though everyone has the "mind of Buddha" and is enlightened; so he left the *Tendai* school. ④*Dōgen* studied under *Myozen*, a disciple of *Eisai*, however, he could not get the answers to his questions.

⑤Consequently, he traveled to China during the Song dynasty to learn Chinese Buddhism. ⑥Studying under the Zen priest *Nyojou*, he attained enlightenment through so called *shikan-taza* (solely sitting). ⑦This means that the true nature of enlightenment is to continue eternal zazen training in quest of the mind of Buddha. ⑧After coming back to Japan, he began to introduce Chinese Zen, but it was not accepted initially. ⑨Soon he

第7章　禅師たちのプロフィール

constructed the first school of Zen in southern Kyoto.
建てた　　　　　　　　　　学校(→道場)
⑩However, it was destroyed by the *Enryaku-ji* temple's priests who were jealous of *Dōgen's* popularity.
　　　　　　　　　　　　　　　　　　　　　　～に嫉妬した　　　　　　　人気
⑪According to the word of *Nyojou*, *Dōgen* decided to
～に従って
withdraw from the authority of the state; he established the
手を引く　　　　　国家権力　　　　　　　　　　　　　　～を建立した
Eihei-ji temple in the mountains of *Echizen* (*Fukui* Pref.).
永平寺

---

66. 道元 (1200~1253)

①幼い道元は、母の死に接して仏教を志し、出家して比叡山の延暦寺に入りました。②道元が学んだ天台宗の思想に、「人間は本来仏性を持っている」ということがありました。③道元は「もともと仏性を持って悟りを開いているのならば、なぜ修行するのか」という疑問を持ち、天台宗から離れていきました。④栄西の弟子の明全に師事しましたが、答えは得られませんでした。⑤そのため道元は中国の仏教を知るために宋に渡りました。⑥如浄という禅僧を師とし、「只管打坐」の悟りを得たのです。⑦それは、仏性を求めて無限の坐禅修行を続けることが、悟りの本質であるということを意味しています。

⑧日本に戻った道元は、中国禅を伝えましたが、最初は受け入れられませんでした。⑨道元は京都南部に日本初の禅道場を建てました。⑩しかし、その寺は道元の人気をねたむ延暦寺僧によって壊されてしまいました。⑪道元は、師の如浄の言葉に従い、国家権力から遠ざかることにし、越前（福井県）の山中に永平寺を建立しました。

67 Ikkyū Sōjun

①*Ikkyū* was born in *Kyōto* as an illegitimate child of Emperor *Gokomatsu* and became a priest at the age of six. ②As a young priest, having inherited his mother's violent moods and intelligence, he could not fit in at the Zen temple, which was corrupted by the overprotection of the Shogunate, in the *Muromachi* period. ③At the age of seventeen, he began studying under *Ken-ō Sōui*. ④After *Sōi*'s death, *Ikkyū* became a disciple of *Kasō Sōdon*. ⑤These two priests greatly influenced him. ⑥*Sōdon* brought out *Ikkyū*'s spirit of defiance.

⑦One night he was floating in a boat on Lake *Biwa*, and hearing a crow cawing in the darkness, he attained enlightenment. ⑧His master, *Sōdon* attempted to give him *Inka* or the certification of enlightenment, however, he refused to accept it. ⑨After the death of *Sōdon*, *Ikkyū* left the temple and traveled everywhere preaching. ⑩At that time, Buddhism was corrupted. ⑪He wrote poetry to protest against Zen temples; and was known for repeating eccentric behaviors. ⑫Later in life, he lived with *Shinjo*, a young, blind female entertainer, and he composed many *waka* poetry in adoration of her. ⑬Being with her, *Ikkyū* deepened his belief and lived freely and easily.

67. 一休 宗純 (1394~1481)

①一休は後小松天皇の私生児として京都に生まれ、6歳で出家しました。②室町時代の当時、幕府に保護されていた禅寺は堕落しており、母親譲りで気性が荒く利発な若い僧の一休は、それになじめませんでした。③そして、17歳のときに謙翁宗為のもとで修行を始めました。④宗為が他界すると、華叟宗曇に入門しました。⑤これら二人の師は一休に大きな影響を与えました。⑥華叟宗曇は一休の反骨精神を引き出しました。
⑦ある夜、一休は闇の中、琵琶湖の船上で烏の鳴き声を聞いて悟りを開きました。⑧師の宗曇は彼に印可を与えようとしましたが、一休は受け取ろうとしませんでした。⑨師の死後は各地を放浪して説法する日々を過ごしました。⑩この時代は、宗教界が堕落していました。⑪一休は、禅寺に抗議する詩を書いたり、風狂な行動を繰り返しました。⑫晩年は、盲目の若い森女という芸人と一緒に暮らし、森女をたたえる歌をたくさん残しました。⑬森女と一休は天衣無縫に暮らし、一休は彼の信念をさらに深めました。

68　*Takuan Sōhō*

①*Takuan*, who was born in *Tajima* (*Hyougo* prefecture), had been the chief priest of the *Daitoku-ji* temple. ②In the beginning of the *Edo* period, the Shogunate strengthened the control of the temples to weaken the relationship between the Emperor and the temples. ③The Shogunate set up a regulation that they nominate the chief priest of the *Daitoku-ji* temple, which was traditionally nominated by the Emperor. ④*Takuan* violently protested against the Shogunate which strengthened the control of the temple. ⑤As a result he was banished to *Dewa* (*Yamagata* pref.). ⑥He was released from the banishment three years later; he accepted *Iemitsu*, the third Shogun of *Tokugawa*, as a believer, and established the *Tokai-ji* temple in *Shinagawa*. ⑦*Takuan* had never given certifications of enlightenment to his disciples. ⑧When he was dying, he wrote to his disciples;

"⑨I don't need disciples to inherit the law of Buddhism, I

第7章　禅師たちのプロフィール

have no need of a posthumous Buddhist name, do not receive
死後につけられた仏教徒の名前(→戒名)
funeral offerings, no funeral ceremony for me, don't cremate
香典　　　　　　　葬式　　　　　　　　　　　　～を火葬にする
my body, bury my body secretly at night, don't visit my
　　　　埋める
grave, no need for a mortuary tablet, and don't recite the
墓　　　　　　　　　位牌　　　　　　　　　　　　　～を唱える
sutra for me." ⑩He hated ornamentation and lived his life as
経　　　　　　　　嫌う　飾り
a true Buddhist.

68. 沢庵 宗彭（たくあん そうほう）（1573~1646）

①沢庵は、但馬（兵庫県）生まれで、大徳寺の前住職の立場（位）を持っている僧侶でした。②江戸時代初期に、幕府は朝廷と寺との関係を弱めるために、寺に対する統制を強めました。③幕府は法度により、従来、天皇の勅命により決められていた大徳寺の住職を、幕府が決めることとしました。④幕府が統制を強化したことに対して、沢庵ははげしく抗議しました。⑤その結果、沢庵は出羽国（山形県）に流されました。

⑥3年後に赦免され、三代将軍家光の帰依を受けた沢庵は、品川に東海寺を開きました。

⑦沢庵は生涯、弟子に印可を与えませんでした。⑧死の間際、弟子たちに次のように書き残しました。⑨「自分の法を嗣ぐ弟子はいらない、禅師号はもらうな、香典は決してもらうな、葬式はしてくれるな、わが身を火葬にするな、夜間こっそり野外に埋めて決してお参りをするな、位牌もいらない、経もあげるな」

⑩沢庵は飾り立てることを嫌い、真の仏道を貫いたのです。

69 Suzuki Shōzan

①*Shōzan*, a priest of the *Sōtō* school, was born in *Mikawa* (*Aichi* pref.). ②He used to be a *samurai* who served *Tokugawa Ieyasu* and *Hidetada*. ③After having experienced combat under the Siege of *Osaka*, he became a priest at the age of forty-two. ④He advocated his original Zen, which is called Zen of Deva Kings. ⑤According to his thought, it is ideal to pray to fierce statues while training; it takes weakness away and makes the heart strong. ⑥He also said that the more you trained, the more you were blessed. ⑦Rather than staying in the temple, *Shozan* wandered from place to place to preach his Zen of Deva Kings. ⑧He also stated that "the way of Buddha" is for each person, whether a *samurai* or a farmer, and each should concentrate on his or her job which had given by heaven. ⑨In other words, Zen is not only the practice of zazen but also concentrating on the job of each individual. ⑩He also thought that all the

第7章 禅師たちのプロフィール

professions are equal under the law of Buddha, although this was during the *Edo* period when a status system of four occupations had been established. ⑪*Shozan*, who was also known as the author of *kana-zōhshi* (books written in *kana*), wrote many stories and made an effort to enlighten common folks with them.

---

69. 鈴木 正三(しょうざん) (1579~1655)

①曹洞宗の僧である正三は、三河(愛知県)に生まれました。②正三は、もともとは徳川家康(いえやす)、秀忠(ひでただ)に仕えた武士でした。③大坂の陣で戦を経験したあと、42歳で出家しました。④正三は独自の禅を唱(とな)え、それは仁王禅(におうぜん)と呼ばれました。⑤正三の考えは、仁王像のような猛々(たけだけ)しい仏像を拝(おが)んで修行に励(はげ)むことで、弱気を追い払い心を強くするというものでした。⑥彼はまた、励めば励むほど心が強くなり、その分、徳が大きくなるとも説(と)きました。⑦正三は、寺の中におさまることなく、諸国を遍歴(へんれき)し、仁王禅を説きました。⑧また、武士であろうが農民であろうが、それぞれ天から与えられた身分や職業に専心することが仏道であると説きました。⑨言い換えれば、坐禅を組むことだけが禅ではなく、それぞれの仕事に打ち込むことがその人の禅だということです。⑩士農工商の身分制度が確立した江戸時代に、彼はすべての職業が仏法のもとに平等であるとしました。
⑪正三は仮名草子(かなぞうし)の作者としても有名で、数々の物語を書き、庶民の教化に努めました。

70 Ingen Ryūki

①*Ingen Ryūki*, who lived in the Ma*npuku-ji* temple of the *Ōbaku* school, was an eminent priest who played an active part in the *Ming* Dynasty. ②During this period, China was in civil disorder because the *Ming* Dynasty had been attacked by the *Qing* Dynasty of northern China. ③*Ingen*, at the age of sixty-three, having accepted an invitation from Japan, immigrated to Japan with many of his disciples. ④Although he had promised to stay in Japan for three years to engage in missionary work at the *Kōfuku-ji* temple in *Nagasaki*, his followers begged him to stay in Japan longer. ⑤*Ingen* was successful in meeting with *Tokugawa Ietsuna*, who granted him a plot of land in *Uji*, *Kyōto*, where he established a temple. ⑥He named this temple *Ōbaku-san Manpuku-ji* after the temple where he had lived in China; here he established the *Ōbaku* school. ⑦Because *Ingen's* teaching of Zen required much more strict training, both the

168

第7章　禅師たちのプロフィール

Rinzai and *Sōtō* schools were greatly influenced by this.

⑧A particular characteristic of the *Ōbaku* school is that the sutra is recited in Chinese. ⑨More than that, many Chinese customs were practiced, as they still are today. ⑩*Ingen* is also known as the priest who brought into Japan, food such as ingen-beans, green tea, and *fucha* meal, which is the Chinese style vegetarian meal for Buddhist.

70. 隠元 隆琦 (1592~1673)

①隠元は、中国の明の時代に活躍した黄檗山萬福寺の高僧でした。②当時の中国は、北方民族の清が明に攻め、混乱していました。③新しい活路を求めて、63歳の隠元は日本の招待に応じ、弟子をたくさん連れて来日しました。④日本に3年間とどまる約束で長崎の興福寺で勤め、多くの信奉者を得ました。⑤将軍徳川家綱に謁見することになった隠元は、家綱から京都の宇治の寺地を賜り、そこに寺を建立しました。⑥隠元はこの寺を、中国の寺にちなんで黄檗山萬福寺と名づけ、黄檗宗を開きました。⑦隠元の禅は、日本の禅よりもずっと戒律が厳しく、臨済宗にも曹洞宗にも大きな影響を与えました。

⑧黄檗宗の特徴は、中国語で読経することです。⑨そのほかにも、中国式の習慣がたくさん残っています。

⑩隠元はインゲン豆、煎茶、中国式の精進料理である普茶料理などを日本にもたらしたことでも知られています。

71 *Hakuin Ekaku*

①*Hakuin* [白隠], born in *Suruga* (*Shizuoka* pref.), became a priest at the age of fifteen, and studied under several masters. ②For a period of time [しばらくの間], when he was disappointed with [〜に失望して] Zen, he wrote texts and poetry. ③The story of a priest, who stuck a needle in [針を突き刺す] his groin [股] to keep from falling asleep [睡眠に落ちないようにする(→眠気を覚ます)] impressed [感動を与えた] him and caused him to [〜に—させる] restart and continue with his study of zazen.

④At the age of eighteen, he attained enlightenment with the *kōan*: "Do dogs have the mind of Buddha?". (see pp.108-109) ⑤After that, he attained grand enlightenment [大悟] under *Dōkyō Etan* [道鏡慧端] of *Shinshu* (*Nagano* Pref.). ⑥However, his strict [厳しい] training caused a Zen disease [病気] which is similar to [〜と同じような] autonomic ataxia [自律神経失調症]. ⑦It caused him to suffer [苦しむ] very much. ⑧He conquered [〜を克服する] it by using "the introspection method" [内観法] that he learned from *Hakuyūshi* [白幽子], a hermit [仙人] living in a cave [洞窟] in the mountains. ⑨*Hakuin* reconstructed [〜をつくり直す] the *kōans*, which originated in China, and adapted them [〜を適応させる] for Japan; making it systematic [体系的な] so as to [〜するために] be easily learned. ⑩After the age of fifty, he established the *Shōin-ji* temple in his home town. ⑪He traveled from here to preach all over the country, and this increased the number of believers. ⑫*Hakuin* was a priest who was filled with the energy to complete everything thoroughly. ⑬Zen pictures of *Bodhidharma* and the Buddha as well as a significant amount of letters and texts from *Hakuin* remain today.

---

71. 白隠 慧鶴（はくいん えかく）(1685~1768)

①白隠は駿河（静岡県）に生まれ、15歳で出家し、いろいろな師につきました。②途中、禅に失望し、詩や文章を書いた時期がありました。③眠気を払うため自分の股に針を刺して坐禅をした僧の物語に感動した白隠は、また各地で修行をしました。

④18歳で、「狗子仏性（犬に仏心はあるか）」の公案（p108～109参照）によって悟りを開きました。⑤その後、信州（長野県）の道鏡慧端禅師のもとで大悟しました。⑥厳しい修行をした白隠は、自律神経失調症のような病気である禅病にかかりました。⑦禅病は、白隠を大変苦しめました。⑧京都で白幽子という仙人に、内観法という心身のリラックス法を学び、その病気を克服しました。

⑨白隠は、中国で生まれた公案を、日本人に合うようにつくり変えたり、学びやすいように体系化しました。⑩50歳をすぎてから、地元に松蔭寺を建てました。⑪そこを本拠地に全国で説法をし、たくさんの信者を得ました。⑫白隠は徹底的にやり抜くエネルギーに満ちた僧でした。⑬膨大な量の書簡や著作と、釈迦や達磨などの禅画を残しています。

72 *Taigu Ryōkan*

①*Ryokan* was born in *Echigo Izumozaki* (*Nigata* Pref.) as a descendant of both a village headman and a Shinto priest. ②At the age of eighteen, when he was working as an apprentice of the village headman, he suddenly became a priest. ③From the age of twenty-two years, he studied in the *Entsu-ji* temple in *Bichū* (*Okayama* pref.) under *Kokusen*. ④After having received certification, he traveled all over the country on foot as a missionary. ⑤When his return to *Echigo* at the age of thirty-eight, he took *Gogōan* monastery as his base, and traveled from place to place; however, he never established a temple during his lifetime. ⑥*Ryokan* lived a stoic life of training. ⑦He lived in a ruinous hut and obtained food only by religious begging. ⑧It is recorded that there were only a desk, a brush and an inkstone in the one room monastery where he was living. ⑨The walls were covered with papers of poems he had written. ⑩Accepting charity, he shared food with those poorer than himself and took the clothes off his

back to give to them. ⑪Some scholars to this day, think that these
actions were a protest against the Zen schools which were corrupt
at the time. ⑫He preached the teachings of the Buddha with
simple words and composed many poems. ⑬He often played with
children and won the sympathy of the people. ⑭He taught the
mind of Zen by example in his own way of living.

72. 大愚 良寛 (1758~1831)

①良寛は、越後出雲崎（新潟県）の名主と神職を兼ねた家の跡取り息子でした。②名主の見習いをしていた18歳のとき、突然出家しました。③22歳から、国仙和尚に師事し、備中（岡山県）の円通寺で修行しました。④印可を受けたあと、全国を行脚して歩きます。⑤38歳で越後に帰りますが、五合庵を中心に転々とし、生涯、寺は設けませんでした。

⑥良寛はストイックな修行生活を送りました。⑦あばら家に住み、托鉢だけで食べ物を得ていました。⑧住まいと寺を兼ねた草庵には、机と筆とすずりしかなかったという記録があります。⑨壁一面には、詩作した紙が貼ってありました。⑩施しを受けるけれども、自分よりも飢えている人には食べ物を分け与え、着物を脱いで渡しました。⑪それは、当時の禅宗の荒廃に対する無言の抗議だったとみる研究家もいます。⑫わかりやすい言葉で仏法を説き、たくさんの歌を詠みました。⑬良寛は子どもとよく遊び、人々の共感を得ました。⑭自身の生き様をありのままに見せることで、禅の心を伝えたのです。

73 *Suzuki Daisetsu*

①In 1893, The World's Congress of Religions was held as a part of the World's Columbian Exposition in Chicago. ②This was the first occasion where men of religion gathered together from around the world. ③At this congress, *Shaku Sōen*, the old master of the *Rinzai* school, delivered a lecture to the world about "The Mind of Zen" for the first time. ④It was young *Daisetu* who translated it into English. ⑤*Daisetsu* had trained in the *Enkaku-ji* temple for four years under the leadership of *Shaku Sōen*. ⑥Then *Daisetsu* went to the United States under the recommendation of *Sōen*, and stayed there for eleven years.

⑦Even after coming back to Japan, he often visited Europe and the United States to deliver lectures and worked hard to spread the teachings of Zen Buddhism to the world, even while he was teaching at *Gakushūin* University and *Ōtani* University. ⑧He also created many works on Zen, such as writing theses and translating sutras. ⑨After the age of eighty, he went to the United

第7章　禅師たちのプロフィール

States again to be a guest professor at Columbia University, where he gave lectures about the ideology of Buddhism. ⑩The ideology of Zen, which *Daisetsu* lectured on, attracted western people and triggered the Zen boom in Western countries. ⑪He expanded awareness of the eastern ideology widely to western society through Zen .

---

73. 鈴木 大拙（だいせつ）（1870~1966）

①1893（明治26）年、シカゴ万国博覧会において「万国宗教会議」が開かれました。②それは全世界の宗教家が初めて一堂に会した会議でした。③ここで、臨済宗の釈宗演（しゃくそうえん）老師が、初めて世界に「禅の心」について講演しました。④この演説を英訳したのが若き日の鈴木大拙です。⑤大拙は釈宗演のもと、円覚寺で4年間の修行をしました。⑥その後、釈宗演のすすめでアメリカに渡り、11年滞在しました。

⑦帰国後は、学習院大学、大谷大学で教鞭（きょうべん）をとりながら、欧米を行き来して講演をし、仏教の普及に尽力（じんりょく）しました。⑧また、数多くの論文の執筆や仏典の英訳も行ないました。⑨80歳をすぎてから、再びアメリカに渡り、コロンビア大学の客員教授になり、仏教思想に関する講義を行ないました。⑩大拙が講義した禅思想は多くの欧米人を魅了し、禅ムーブメントが起こりました。⑪大拙は、禅を通して東洋の思想を西洋社会に広く知らしめたのです。

People Influenced by Zen / 禅の影響を受けた人々⑤

Steve Jobs　スティーブ・ジョブズ

Steve Jobs, who was interested in oriental thought when he was young, met Master *Otukawa Kōbun* of the *Sōtō* school. At the time, Zen was spreading in the United States, especially among the people known as the "Beat Generation", who pursued spirituality. Jobs was one of them.

In 2005, having just recovered from pancreatic cancer, he gave a significant speech to the students of Stanford University. "Your time is limited, so don't waste it living someone else's life. Don't be trapped by dogma--which is living with the results of other people's thinking." At the end of the speech he quoted a phrase from a magazine which he had loved when he was young; "Stay Hungry. Stay Foolish." He emphasized it three times. This phrase certainly describes the "mind of Zen".

東洋思想に興味を持っていた若き日のジョブズは、曹洞宗の禅僧の乙川弘文と出会いました。当時のアメリカでは、「ビートジェネレーション」と呼ばれる精神世界を追求する人々の間で、禅が広がっていました。ジョブズもそうした若者の一人でした。

2005年、すい臓がんから再起したジョブズは、スタンフォード大学で学生たちに、すばらしいスピーチをしました。「あなたの時間は限られている。だから、他人の人生を生きて、時間を無駄にしてはいけない。他人が出した結論で生きるという罠にはまってはいけない」。最後にジョブズは、若い頃に愛読した雑誌の言葉を引用しました。「ハングリーであれ、愚かであれ」。ジョブズはこの言葉を力を込めて3回繰り返しました。この言葉は、禅の心を表しているといえます。

Chapter 8

Zen and Japanese Culture

第8章
禅と日本文化の関わり

Zen Buddhism

74 Zen and Japanese Art

①Zen Buddhism has influenced various fields of Japanese art such as architecture, painting, garden design and the tea ceremony. ②Some of them were imported with Zen Buddhism from China, and others originated in Japan. ③All of them developed independently in Japan during the *Kamakura* period and flourished in the *Muromachi* period.

④Brush painting called "*Suiboku-ga*" or "Wash painting" is a technique which had developed in China from the *Tang* Dynasty to the *Song* Dynasty, and was introduced to Japan by the Chinese priests immigrating into Japan. ⑤Most of the famous painters in this period are Zen priests. ⑥*Sesshū*, a prominent painter of this style, was a Zen priest, who studied painting for three years in China and established his own style afterward.

⑦The tea ceremony originated in Japan. ⑧There were various styles of tea parties during the *Muromachi* period, which were predecessors for the tea ceremony. ⑨For example: people would

第8章 禅と日本文化の関わり

guess the production area of teas and gamble on it; a feudal lord would buy expensive tea cups imported from abroad and would then hold tea parties to show them off. ⑩It was *Murata Shukō* who organized the tea ceremony in which people valued spiritual connections. ⑪These arts influenced by Zen are regarded as the cornerstones of Japanese modern art.

74. 禅と芸術

①禅は、建築、絵画、庭園デザイン、茶の湯など、日本の芸術等に影響を与えてきました。②それらの中には、中国から渡来したものと、日本で生まれたものがあります。③どちらも、鎌倉時代から室町時代にかけて、日本で独自の発展を遂げました。④水墨画と呼ばれる画法は、中国で唐から宋の時代に発達し、中国から日本に渡来した禅僧たちによって、日本にもたらされました。⑤この時代に名を成した画家のほとんどは禅僧でした。⑥水墨画の著名な画家である雪舟は、3年間中国で絵画の修行をしたのちに、日本で独自の作風をうち立てました。

⑦茶の湯は、日本で生まれました。⑧室町時代には、茶の湯に先立って、さまざまな形の茶会がありました。⑨たとえば、茶の産地を当てる賭けごととしての茶会、あるいは、大名が高級な茶器を輸入し、お披露目のために開催する茶会などです。⑩精神性を重んじるものとしての茶の湯は、村田珠光が体系づけたものです。⑪これらの、禅によって影響を受けた諸芸術は、日本の現代芸術の礎となったと考えられています。

75 Tea Ceremony

① Tea was imported into Japan during the *Nara* period.
② Since the end of the *Heian* period, the custom of drinking tea had spread widely over the country. ③ It was *Eisai* who imported tea tree seeds and began the custom of drinking tea, which had originally been the custom of Chinese Zen temples. ④ A work of *Eisai*, "Be Healthy with Drinking Tea" or "*Kissa Yōjōki*" urged the spread of the custom to the *samurai* society. ⑤ In the *Muromachi* period, a Zen priest, *Murata Shukō* merged the custom of drinking tea with the "mind of Zen", which he had learned from *Ikkyū*. ⑥ *Sen-no-rikyū*, the father of the modern tea ceremony was descended from *Shukō*. ⑦ After having learned the "mind of Zen" at the *Daitoku-ji* temple, *Sen-no-rikyū* removed the superfluous and constructed simple tea rooms, in the pursuit of the spirit of "the Combination of Zen and Tea". ⑧ "Meeting only once in a lifetime", which was written by

Yamanoue Sōji, a disciple of *Sen-no-rikyū*, is well-known. ⑨This means: "I will only meet you once in my life, so I will always give you the very best service as warmly as I can." ⑩This phrase expresses one aspect of the idea of Zen very well. ⑪Therefore, the tea ceremony and Zen, culturally and historically, have had strong relationships.

75. 茶道

①茶は、奈良時代に中国から渡来しました。
②茶を飲む習慣が本格的に広がったのは、平安時代の末頃からです。③中国から茶の木の種を持ち帰り、禅寺の飲茶の習慣を日本に伝えたのは、栄西です。
④栄西が著した『喫茶養生記』によって、茶を飲む習慣は武家社会に広まりましました。⑤室町時代になると、禅僧の村田珠光が、茶の習慣と一休から受け継いだ禅の精神を融合しました。
⑥現代の茶道の父と呼ばれる千利休は、村田珠光の流れをくんでいます。⑦千利休は大徳寺で禅の精神を学び、贅沢を廃して簡素な茶室を設けるなど、「茶禅一味」の精神を深く追求しました。⑧千利休の弟子の山上宗二の著作に出てくる「一期一会」は、よく知られた言葉です。⑨「あなたと出会っているこの時間は、一生に一度きりで二度とはないのですから、今できる最高のおもてなしをします」という意味です。⑩この言葉は、禅の考え方の一つの側面をよく表しています。⑪このように、禅と茶道は歴史的にも文化的にも深い関わりを持っています。

76　Zen and the Swordsmanship

① Swordplay had been developed as the skill for fighting.
② It was *Yagyū Munenori* who adopted the idea of Zen as the foundation of the spirit of swordplay.
③ *Munenori* was born the fifth son of *Yagyū Muneyoshi*, one of the eminent swordsman certificated by the Shogunate. ④ He fought actively in the Battle of *Sekigahara* where *Tokugawa Ieyasu* captured the Shogunate. ⑤ Because of his outstanding performance in the battle, *Munenori* was appointed as the instructor of *Tokugawa Hidetada*, the second *Shōgun* of *Tokugawa*, and afterwards, of *Tokugawa Iemitsu*, the third *Shōgun*.

⑥ It is well known that *Munenori* had a strong relationship with Master *Takuan*(see p.164). ⑦ It is said that *Munenori* recommended *Takuan* as the religious adviser of *Iemitsu* when *Takuan* was released from exile.
⑧ *Takuan* wrote many letters to *Munenori* in which he

第8章 禅と日本文化の関わり

referred to the similarities between Zen and swordplay, and
言及した 　　　　類似性(→共通点)
discussed the spirit of the martial arts through the "mind of
　　　　　　　　　　　　　　　武道
Zen". ⑨The words described in the letters, "Sword and Zen
　　　　　　　　　記述された
are perfectly the same" or "*kenzen itinyo*", have been
　　　　　　　　　　　　　　　　剣禅一如
regarded as intrinsic to Japanese swordsmanship.
見なされる　　本質的な　　　　　　　　　　剣道

76. 禅と剣の道

①剣術は戦いの手段として発達してきました。②そこに、精神のよりどころとして禅の考え方を取り入れたのは柳生宗矩でした。
③宗矩は、徳川家から印可状を与えられた高名な剣術家である柳生宗厳の五男として生まれました。④そして、徳川家康が天下をとった関ヶ原の戦いで活躍しました。⑤この戦いでのめざましい活躍により、宗矩は二代目将軍・徳川秀忠の剣術師範になり、後に三代目将軍・徳川家光の師範になりました。
⑥宗矩が沢庵和尚（p164参照）とごく親しい関係にあったことは、よく知られています。⑦沢庵が流罪から解放されたときに、家光に心の師として沢庵を推挙したのは、宗矩だったともいわれています。
⑧沢庵は宗矩にあてて送った多くの書簡の中で、禅と剣術の共通点に言及し、禅を通して武道の精神を論じています。⑨この書簡の中にある「剣禅一如」という言葉は、日本の剣術の精神面での一つの基本とされています。

77   Japanese Calligraphy

①Japanese calligraphy originated as the writing of symbols imported from China, in black ink, with a brush. ②In the *Heian* period when *hiragana* was invented, the style of Japanese calligraphy changed from masculine and powerful to feminine and soft. ③After a time, in the *Muromachi* period, many Chinese Zen priests immigrated into Japan with their style of calligraphy, and the powerful style of the Chinese calligraphy became mainstream again.

④The calligraphy of Zen priests is called "*bokuseki*". ⑤Most of the priests, loving calligraphy, expressed their feelings in Chinese style poems. ⑥Their calligraphy, drawn freely without using a particular technique, is unique and tasteful.

⑦As the tea ceremony became popular with the people, the works of Zen priests began to be displayed in the tea ceremony rooms. ⑧Among them, you may find scroll

calligraphy in which only one circle is drawn. ⑨One of the
掛け軸になっている書　　　　　　　　　　　円
interpretations about this circle is that it is a calligraphy
解釈
which symbolizes the four important
　　　　　象徴化する
factors of Zen: enlightenment, truth,
要素
the "nature of Buddha" and the

universe.

一円相

77. 書道

①日本の書道は、中国から筆とともに入ってきた漢字を墨(すみ)で書くことから始まりました。②平安時代にひらがながつくられると、それまでの男性的で力強い書風は女性的でやわらかいものへと変化しました。③やがて室町時代になり、禅僧が多く渡来するようになると、力強い中国の書風がふたたび主流になりました。④禅僧の書は墨蹟(ぼくせき)と呼ばれています。⑤禅僧は、よく書に親しみ、心情を漢詩で表しました。⑥禅僧の書は技巧にとらわれずに自由に書き、自分の心境を素直に表したものであり、個性的で味わいがあります。

⑦茶道が広く親しまれるようになると、禅僧の書が茶室の床(とこ)の間(ま)に飾られるようになりました。⑧そうした禅僧の書の中には、文字ではなく、ただ円が描かれているものがあります。⑨この円は、禅の四つの大切な要素である「悟り」、「真理」、「仏性」、「宇宙」を象徴的に表現している、などと解釈されています。

78　Wash Painting

① Wash painting is the technique of drawing in which the object is depicted using the contrast of black ink. ② This technique, having been developed from the *Tang* to the *Song* Dynasty in China, was brought to Japan by Zen priests.

『瓢鮎図』如拙 筆（生没年不詳）
"Catching a cat fish with a Gourd" Josetsu (years unknown)

「瓢箪で鮎が獲れるか」という公案を題材にした、如拙の画。

Drawing by *Josetsu* which depicts the *kōan* "Can a fisher catch a cat fish with Gourd?"

[如心寺退蔵院（京都）所蔵]

『竹斎読書図』周文 筆 （1414-1463）
"Reading in a Bamboo Grove" Shūbun

雪舟の師に当たる周文は、室町時代に水墨画を確立させた禅僧。

Shubun, the teacher of *Sesshu*, is a Zen priest who established wash painting in the *Muromachi* period.

[東京国立博物館　所蔵]

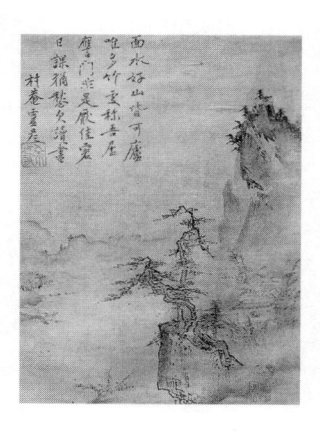

第8章　禅と日本文化の関わり

78. 水墨画(すいぼくが)

①水墨画は、黒い墨の濃淡を利用して描く絵画技法です。②この技法は唐から宋の時代にかけて中国で発達し、渡来した禅僧によって日本に伝えられました。

『達磨図(だるまず)』白隠(はくいん) 筆
（1685-1768）

"Bodhidharma" Hakuin

白隠は多くの達磨図や釈迦図を描いた（p170 参照）。

Hakuin drew many portraits of *Bodhidharma* and *Gautama Siddhārtha* (see p.170).

[所蔵不明]

『慧可断臂図(えかだんびず)』雪舟(せっしゅう) 筆
（1420-1506）

"Bodhidharma and Huike (Eka)" Sesshu

慧可は自分の左手を切断して、入門の決意を達磨に見せた故事（p40 参照）を描いた作品。

This picture is of the story about *Bodhidharma* and *Eka*; *Eka* cut off his left arm and showed his determination to become a disciple of *Bodhidharma* (see p.40).

[京都国立博物館　所蔵]

『蝦蟇仙人図(がまセんにんず)』蕭白(しょうはく) 筆
（1730-1781）

"Toad Hermit" Shōhaku

蕭白は「異端・狂気」の画家といわれた。濃い墨や太い線を用いた白隠の影響を受けたとされる。

Shohaku was regarded as miscreant and eccentric painter. He was influenced by *Hakuin* who drew with dense ink and with thick lines.

[ボストン美術館　所蔵]

187

79　Zen Garden

①The style of gardens in the Zen temples is known as "*Zen tei*". ②This style was established during the *Kamakura* period, when Zen Buddhism merged with the traditional Japanese gardens and developed into the gardens of Zen temples. ③The characteristics of the style are simple, stoic and abstract. ④In this style, all aspects of nature, such as mountains, rivers or even the universe, are expressed with inorganic materials such as sand, rocks and stones.

⑤The Zen garden is divided into several styles. ⑥The Japanese rock gardens, or "*Kare-sansui*" is the best known among them. ⑦For example, the garden of *Daisen-in* of the *Daitoku-ji* temple, *Kyōto*, is designed in this style. ⑧There, a waterfall cascading from a mountain and a river flowing into the ocean are conceptualized with white sand; cranes and turtles, which are symbols of long life in Japan, are conceptualized with rocks.

⑨ *Musō Soseki*, a Zen priest of the *Muromachi* period is one of the leading garden designers in this period. ⑩ The garden of the *Saihō-ji* temple and of the *Tenryū-ji* temple are two of his works that still remain. ⑪ They are registered on the World Heritage List and retain the same features as when they were originally constructed.

---

79. 禅庭

①禅寺の庭園様式は、禅庭として知られています。②この様式は、鎌倉時代に日本古来の伝統的な庭園と禅が融合して確立し、禅寺の庭園様式として発展しました。

③この様式の特徴は、質素で禁欲的で抽象的なことです。④この様式では、山、川、そして宇宙といった自然の風景が、砂、岩、石などの無機的な素材で表現されます。⑤禅庭の様式はいくつかに分かれています。⑥中でも一番知られているのは「枯山水」です。⑦たとえば、京都の大徳寺大仙院の庭園は、この枯山水の様式で造られています。⑧そこでは、山から落ちる滝、海に流れ込む水をすべて白い砂で、また長寿の鶴亀を岩で表現しています。

⑨室町時代に、多くの禅宗の庭園をデザインした禅僧が夢窓疎石です。⑩京都の西芳寺と天龍寺の庭園は、夢窓疎石の手によるもので、現在でも残っています。⑪これらの庭園は世界遺産に指定されて、造られたときと同じ姿をとどめています。

80　Buddhist Cuisine

①In Mahayana Buddhism, of which Japanese and Chinese Buddhism are components, eating meat is forbidden. ②This is the reason vegetarian cuisine was developed in the temples in China. ③Vegetarian food was thought to be imported into Japan with Buddhism in the fifth century and was called *shōjin* cuisine. ④However, it was far afterward in the *Kamakura* period that vegetarian food became popular here. ⑤When Zen Buddhism was flourishing, vegetarian food was served in the temples as daily meals for the priests. ⑥*Dōgen*(see p.160), an eminent priest in the beginning of the *Kamakura* period wrote two texts about cooking, "*Tenzo Kyōkun*" and "*Fushuku Hanpō*", which are regarded as the fundamentals of *Shōjin* cuisine. ⑦In "*Tenzo Kyōkun*", cooking methods such as treatment of material and seasoning is explained in detail. ⑧On the other hand, in the text, "*Fushuku Hanpō*", it is the manner of eating that is

described.
書かれている

⑨There is another style of Buddhist vegetarian cuisine called "*Fucha cuisine*", which was imported into Japan from China by Master *Ingen*(see p.168). ⑩Compared to *shōjin* cuisine, *Fucha* cuisine retains a Chinese flavor and stands out because of its brighter colors.

普茶料理 / 隠元 / ～と比べて / ～を残す / らしさ / 際立つ / より鮮やかな

---

80. 精進料理

①日本や中国の仏教が属する大乗仏教では、肉食が禁じられていました。②そのため、中国の寺では菜食の料理が発達しました。③そうした菜食料理は、5世紀に仏教とともに日本に伝来し、精進料理と呼ばれるようになったと考えられています。④しかし、日本でそれが普及したのは、ずっとあとの鎌倉時代になってからのことでした。⑤禅宗が盛んになると、菜食料理は僧たちの食事として寺でふるまわれるようになりました。

⑥鎌倉時代初期の高名な僧である道元（p160参照）は、食事に関して『典座教訓』と『赴粥飯法』を書き、これらが精進料理の基本だと考えられています。⑦『典座教訓』では、素材の扱い方や味つけについて、詳細にわたり解説されています。⑧一方、『赴粥飯法』では、食事のマナーなどが解説されています。

⑨精進料理のほかに、隠元（p168参照）によって日本にもたらされた普茶料理と呼ばれる菜食料理があります。⑩普茶料理は精進料理に比べて中華料理らしさが残り、鮮やかな色彩が特徴となっています。

監修者

尾関宗園（おぜき そうえん）

1932年、奈良市生まれ。奈良教育大学卒業。
1965年、33歳の若さで京都大徳寺大仙院住職となり、2007年より閑栖。
高齢を感じさせない豪快さと迫力がある一方で、やさしくユーモアにあふれたその語り口は人々に生きる力と自信を与えている。
主な著書は、『生きてるうちに大往生』（実業之日本社）、『新・いま頑張らずにいつ頑張る!』（日新報道）、『あんたが一番えらいんや!』（ロングセラーズ）、『一日一禅』（徳間書店）ほか、多数ある。

【連絡先】
臨済宗大徳寺派　大徳寺塔頭　大仙院
〒603-8231　京都市北区紫野大徳寺町54-1
TEL　075-491-8346（9〜16時30分まで）
URL　https://daisen-in.net/

英文監訳者

Elizabeth Mills（エリザベス・ミルズ）

米国シアトル（ワシントン州）生まれ。
セントラルワシントン大学卒業。
セントラルキットサップスクールにて18年間、教師を務める。現在、日本で生活。
日本人の母とアメリカ人の父を持ち、日本の歴史・しきたり・文化等に造詣が深い。

じっぴコンパクト新書　079

むずかしい教えがスッキリわかる!
英語対訳で読む禅入門
Introduction to Zen

2011年4月23日　初版第1刷発行
2023年1月20日　初版第6刷発行

監修者	尾関宗園
英文監訳者	Elizabeth Mills
発行者	岩野裕一
発行所	株式会社実業之日本社

〒107-0062 東京都港区南青山5-4-30
emergence aoyama complex 3F
電話（編集）03-6809-0452　（販売）03-6809-0495
実業之日本社のホームページ　https://www.j-n.co.jp/

印刷・製本　大日本印刷株式会社

©Studio Spark 2011 Printed in Japan
ISBN978-4-408-10890-2（第一経済）

本書の一部あるいは全部を無断で複写・複製（コピー、スキャン、デジタル化等）・転載することは、法律で定められた場合を除き、禁じられています。
また、購入者以外の第三者による本書のいかなる電子複製も一切認められておりません。
落丁・乱丁（ページ順序の間違いや抜け落ち）の場合は、ご面倒でも購入された書店名を明記して、小社販売部あてにお送りください。送料小社負担でお取り替えいたします。
ただし、古書店等で購入したものについてはお取り替えできません。
定価はカバーに表示してあります。
小社のプライバシー・ポリシー（個人情報の取り扱い）は上記ホームページをご覧ください。